THE
APOLLO
ADVENTURE

"Inside this fine book by Jeffrey Kluger is an interesting compilation of both what we as a creative team learned about the glorious days of the entire Apollo era and what occurred in making a movie about its thirteenth mission. While I learned a lot, I know I came away from the experience with one belief firmly intact: not only should our world's space explorers be honored by us all for their accomplishments, but by examining and celebrating what they achieved, we also acknowledge something important about our own spirit."

—from the Foreword by Ron Howard

THE
APOLLO
ADVENTURE

The Making of the
Apollo Space Program
and
the Movie *Apollo 13*

Jeffrey Kluger

with a foreword by
RON HOWARD

POCKET BOOKS
New York   London   Toronto   Sydney   Tokyo   Singapore

Also by Jeffrey Kluger

Apollo 13 (*with Jim Lovell*)
  [*previously published as* Lost Moon]

Available from POCKET BOOKS

Unless otherwise indicated, photos in this book were taken by Ron Batzdorff, Robert Markowitz, or Michael Garland.

An *Original* Publication of POCKET BOOKS

POCKET BOOKS, a division of Simon & Schuster Inc.
1230 Avenue of the Americas, New York, NY 10020

Library of Congress Catalog Card Number: 95-069195

ISBN 0-671-53542-0

First Pocket Books trade paperback printing July 1995

10 9 8 7 6 5 4 3 2 1

DESIGN: Stanley S. Drate/Folio Graphics Co., Inc.

Dedicated, in mission order, to Frank Borman, Jim Lovell, Bill Anders, Tom Stafford, John Young, Gene Cernan, Neil Armstrong, Mike Collins, Buzz Aldrin, Pete Conrad, Dick Gordon, Alan Bean, Jack Swigert, Fred Haise, Al Shepard, Stu Roosa, Ed Mitchell, Dave Scott, Al Worden, Jim Irwin, Ken Mattingly, Charlie Duke, Ron Evans, and Jack Schmitt: the men who made the trip

CONTENTS

Ron Howard and Tom Hanks in front of the movie's Mission Control screen.

FOREWORD
by Ron Howard

My rental-house phone rang and then kept ringing. My family had moved into the place only a couple of days before, and we were settling in for the New York City production of what would be my next film, *The Paper*. It wasn't that late, maybe nine-fifteen or so, but the kids were asleep and my wife, Cheryl, and I wanted to be. I wasn't even sure where this phone was, but the ringing led me through a pile of clutter and finally to the source. The voice on the other end was a familiar and always welcome one: my friend and business partner at Imagine Films for the past decade or so, producer Brian Grazer. Brian and I routinely talk several times a day, but for him to call me after 9 P.M. had to mean something important was under way.

"There's this book," Brian began, "well, it's not even a book yet, it's a ten-page outline written by Jeff Kluger and James Lovell. Lovell is the astronaut who was commander on Apollo 13. Do you remember that flight?"

I stared at the ceiling and tried to assign some significance to that mission, but at that moment I was coming up with zip. "I guess I don't," I finally admitted.

"I didn't either, but the story sounds like something you might be interested in directing. It's completely different from anything you've done, and producers and studios are starting to bid on it, so I wanted to put you in the loop on this one."

Brian has a great way of distilling any movie-business situation into a couple of sentences that pretty much say it all. My curiosity was piqued, and Brian and Imagine Films vice president Michael Bostick went on to tell me about the true story of the ill-fated Apollo 13 mission, which I did finally begin to recall rather hazily. In April of 1970, commander Jim Lovell and his copilots, Jack Swigert and Fred Haise, were on their way out to the moon for the third planned lunar landing when an oxygen-tank explosion crippled their main spacecraft, known as their command-service module. For four days, the crew had to use their attached lunar module as a lifeboat, but the lunar module was principally designed to land on the moon and could only keep two men alive for two days. Now, three men were aboard and they would have to survive in the craft for the more than half-week journey home. The story was far more compelling and suspenseful than I had remembered.

Bostick had an advantage in recalling this little-remembered true story since his father, Jerry, had been on the Mission Control team in Houston that had worked around the clock dealing with the crisis in space. Michael described the events in emotional, human, and dramatic terms, and when our conversation was over, both Brian and I agreed that a strong movie could indeed be made out of this story. We determined to join the bidding for the book.

After four long hours of negotiating, which culminated in a deal-closing conference call at around 1 A.M. my time, we succeeded in gaining the rights. Whew! I celebrated by rolling over and going to sleep, then didn't think too much more about Apollo 13 until a few months later when I had the first unforgettable meeting with Jim Lovell at our Imagine Films offices in Los Angeles.

As I sat at the conference table listening to the extraordinary yet accessible Captain Lovell talk about how he and his compatriots had barely survived their near-disastrous journey, I realized that this story would need no Hollywoodizing. Instead, the power and entertainment value lay in the detailed truth of this amazing human adventure. In fact, the more I learned about the twists and turns of this adventure, the more excited I got about the story.

"I'm glad this is documentable," I remember thinking, "because no one would believe a lot of this stuff if it hadn't really happened."

I also sensed as a filmmaker that to do this story justice, I would have to begin a process of research and discovery that would encompass both the Apollo 13 mission and the space program as a whole. I knew so little about the subject, and yet this movie would provide an opportunity not only to bring a great American story to the screen, but also to reflect on an incredible era in our history. A bunch of human beings, with all our natural limitations and with primitive technology at our disposal, still managed to stretch our resources and capabilities to the max and make unparalleled advances in manned exploration of space. My goal as a moviemaker would be to take audiences *on* that adventure—to allow moviegoers to feel a little bit of what it was like twenty-five years ago to brave the vacuum of space and literally go where no man had gone before.

Ron Howard, holding a copy of *Lost Moon* by Jim Lovell and Jeff Kluger, directing the liftoff scene in *Apollo 13.*

A number of important breakthroughs were made over the following months that paved the way for what proved to be an extraordinary moviemaking experience. First, Bill Broyles, a renowned journalist, author, and screen and television writer, agreed to write the screenplay in collaboration with his old friend and fellow journalist Al Reinert. Al was responsible for the wonderful compilation documentary film about the Apollo era, *For All Mankind,* a mustsee movie for anyone interested in real-life space travel. They began the formidable work of shaping the story into a movie that would run a couple of hours or so. This was tough, since so many of the details of this mission as recorded in various accounts as well as in Lovell and Kluger's excellent book were dramatic, exciting, and entertaining. What could we stand to leave out when it was all so rich and interesting? Bill and Al did their work well and, along with a valuable assist from John Sayles during the rewrite phase of preproduction, gave us a strong script to work with.

Another key collaborator in the process was Tom Hanks. I was thrilled to learn of his interest in the project (particularly since I had directed Tom in his first feature film, *Splash,* and had been looking for an opportunity to work with him again ever since), and when Tom and I met in New York about it, I

The original members of the prime crew, in December 1969, of the Apollo 13 lunar-landing mission. From left to right: astronauts James A. Lovell Jr., commander; Thomas K. Mattingly II, command module pilot; and Fred W. Haise Jr., lunar module pilot. *(NASA)*

saw that he had a long-standing love affair with the space program and had always been particularly interested in the story of Apollo 13. Due to his passion for all things NASA, he was miles ahead of me in knowledge of the basics of space flight and the details of the mission. I would be lying if I said I have caught up with Tom. His knowledge, enthusiasm, and artistry made him a huge contributor, beyond his wonderful performance as James Lovell. What a pleasure to be directing Tom Hanks!

I had never before felt so inspired by the people I met during the research for any of my projects. In addition to James Lovell, I met Apollo 13 lunar-module pilot Fred Haise, as well as Ken Mattingly, who had been bumped from the Apollo 13 mission a few days before the flight after being exposed to the measles. Mattingly went on to earn high marks from everyone I spoke to for his diligent work in Houston on the rescue effort.

Other Apollo astronauts we had a chance to meet along the way included

Dave Scott (who worked arduously as a technical adviser for us throughout the filming and, by the way, was the first man to drive a moon buggy on the lunar surface), Ed Gibson (who helped us out with some advice on a couple of shooting days), John Young (who actually honored us by taking us for a ride in a shuttle simulator—awesome!), Al Bean (who is now a fine artist as well as a great conversationalist with a wealth of space-flight information to share), Eugene Cernan (the last man to set foot on the moon), Pete Conrad (third man to set foot on the moon, Skylab pioneer, and a great, great storyteller), and Buzz Aldrin (lunar-module pilot on the first moon landing, second man to set foot on the moon, and by all accounts, one of the great minds in NASA's history).

In addition, I had the honor of meeting and talking to around a dozen shuttle astronauts, and witnessing a remarkable and (for me) emotional shuttle launch in the spring of 1994. We were also able to orchestrate an incredible reunion of many of the mission controllers from Apollo 13 in the actual Mission Control room, including Chris Kraft, one of the space agency's founders, and flight directors Glynn Lunney and Gene Kranz. The insights we gained from that afternoon and evening had a huge impact on our movie.

Actors Tom Hanks, Kevin Bacon, and Bill Paxton in the earth-bound lunar module in one g. In reality, the camera is on its side and the actors are on bellyboards.

Jim Lovell and his family in March 1970. From left to right: Barbara, Marilyn, Jeffrey, Jim, and Susan. *(NASA)*

The eventual prime crew, in April 1970, of Apollo 13. From left to right: James A. Lovell Jr., commander; John L. Swigert Jr., command module pilot; and Fred W. Haise Jr., lunar module pilot. *(NASA)*

Director Ron Howard and actor Gary Sinise in Mission Control.

Jim Lovell before the
launch of Apollo 13.
(NASA)

Gerry Griffin and Jerry Bostick, both veteran mission controllers, aided us tremendously in authentically bringing to life the dramatic intensity of the Mission Control room during the Apollo crisis.

In making the movie I had the second-most-incredible experience of my life (the first was witnessing the birth of my children): flying and filming in NASA's KC-135 zero-gravity simulator, also known as the Vomit Comet. This is a plane that flies in a parabolic arc between the altitudes of 30,000 and 36,000 feet, creating weightlessness inside the aircraft for around twenty-three weird seconds per parabola. No, that "weightless room" we all think we have heard about is nothing but a myth, but the Vomit Comet is, believe me, absolutely real and as wild as it gets. As far as filming goes, it is totally disorienting but the only way to truly re-create zero g for the purposes of making a realistic movie about space travel. Thanks to NASA's willingness to allow us access to this plane and its test directors, as well as the mental and physical toughness of the actors and crew, we had the rides of our lives and got some unprecedented motion-picture scenes to boot.

Inside this fine book by Jeffrey Kluger is an interesting compilation of both what we as a creative team learned about the glorious days of the entire Apollo era and what occurred in making a movie about its thirteenth mission. While I learned a lot, I know I came away from the experience with one belief firmly intact: not only should our world's space explorers be honored by us all for their accomplishments, but by examining and celebrating what they achieved, we also acknowledge something important about our own spirit.

We should not remember the astronauts and engineers who led us to the moon as a bunch of recklessly heroic types who did something amazing back in the sixties and early seventies that will never be repeated again. Rather, we should remember them merely as the *first* to go. With all of humanity's other needs that must be addressed, we should not overlook that which makes us different from all of the other inhabitants of planet Earth: our need to know.

Sometimes when I ask myself that ultimate big question—"What are we here for anyway?"—a part of me surmises that the answer might lie in our natural inclination to wonder what is over the next hill, across that body of water, or beyond our own galaxy; and in our tendency—when we simply cannot stand to wonder about it any longer—to risk it all and go find out. Maybe that is, indeed, our calling.

What do you think?

PROLOGUE

The Remarkable Fraternity dwindled a little more last December. Actually, it lost only one member, but when you're down to twenty-one to begin with, the loss of yet another name hurts a lot.

At first, of course, there were an even two dozen honorees included in the Fraternity's membership rolls—the rolls on which the names of the Apollo lunar astronauts were recorded. But in 1982, Jack Swigert died; in 1990, Ron Evans followed him; in 1991, Jim Irwin went too. Last December, Stu Roosa joined those three, reducing the roster of the Remarkable Fraternity to just twenty men.

There was a time when the death of Stu Roosa would have been the stuff of headlines. In the early 1970s, the memory of the spectacular things he had accomplished during one magnificent week was still fresh in people's minds. On January 31, 1971, Roosa, along with his friends and crewmates Al Shepard and Ed Mitchell, set off on a journey to the Fra Mauro highlands of the moon. Less than four days later, Shepard and Mitchell set their fragile, bug-like lunar lander down on the soil of the ancient hills, while Roosa remained orbiting overhead, station-keeping in the trusty command module.

Even in 1971, Shepard, Roosa, and Mitchell's flight—designated Apollo 14—did not get all the attention it deserved, mostly because it was not the first mission to attempt such a preposterous journey. Apollos 8, 10, and 13 had already visited the lunar neighborhood. Apollos 11 and 12 had already landed on the surface of the moon. Fourteen men had been aboard the ships that made those trips, and one of them—Jim Lovell—had been aboard two. What's more, with up to a dozen moon flights planned in the entire Apollo program, and who knew how many more in the dreamed-of colonization of the moon that would almost surely follow, the number of people who traveled the translunar highway would mushroom. Frank Borman, Jim Lovell, and Bill Anders might be remembered as the pilots of the first mission to orbit the distant body; Neil Armstrong, Mike Collins, and Buzz Aldrin might be remembered as the first to fly a landing mission. After that, however, the fraternity—and indeed, the sorority—of lunar travelers would swell to the point of near-anonymity.

But the fraternity remained a fraternity, and it never did swell much. Apollo 20, which was to have been the crowning flight in this first round of lunar expeditions, was canceled due to budget cuts. Apollos 19 and 18 soon followed suit.

The idea of subsequent colonization missions was consigned to the realm of fantasy. In December 1972, less than a week before the solstice—the shortest and literally the least enlightened day of the year—Gene Cernan, the commander of Apollo 17, climbed into his lunar module, lit his ascent engine, and blasted off from the moon's Taurus-Littrow highlands, concluding a program of otherworldly exploration that had begun just four years earlier.

More than a generation later, the artifacts of the age of lunar expeditions remain. The mammoth 36-story Saturn 5 booster that was to have launched Apollo 18 lies on the ground, gutted and whale-like, at the front entrance of the Johnson Space Center in Houston. An identical booster, intended for Apollo 19, lies in a similarly taxidermic state at Cape Canaveral. Tour guides at the two facilities invite visitors to walk the length of the giant artifacts, referring proudly to the twin rockets as two of the Agency's most popular attractions. Employees, many of them veterans of the Apollo era, refer to them as "lawn ornaments" when somebody inquires about the boosters: "Four-hundred-million-dollar lawn ornaments." Up on the moon, the descent stages of the Apollo 11, 12, 14, 15, 16, and 17 lunar modules have spent the last twenty-plus years in even more-pristine condition—undisturbed by wind, unrusted by rain, perhaps a bit pitted by the occasional micrometeorite. On the front leg of Apollo 11's module is a plaque commemorating the first lunar landing. On the front leg of Apollo 17's module is a similar plaque commemorating the last. It reads:

> HERE MAN COMPLETED HIS FIRST EXPLORATIONS
> OF THE MOON. MAY THE SPIRIT OF PEACE IN WHICH
> WE CAME BE REFLECTED IN THE LIVES OF
> ALL MANKIND.

Originally, the second sentence of the plaque was to have read "WE WILL COME AGAIN IN PEACE FOR ALL MANKIND," but on November 22, 1972, just weeks before the launch, the order came down from NASA and the White

House that the inscription was to be amended to include the less-ambitious phrasing. Evidently, neither the administration nor the space agency wanted to make any promises they couldn't keep.

But if the nation lost both the will and the wallet to fly to the moon, it did not lose its appreciation of the men and machines responsible for making the trips. The supine Saturn 5s in Florida and Texas and the six abandoned LEMs in the soil of the moon may be forlorn monuments, but they are monuments nonetheless. Around the world, other artifacts—the pod-like command modules the teams of astronauts piloted; the now-dingy, dirt-stained pressure suits they wore; the precious, priceless rocks they traveled a quarter of a million miles to gather—are enshrined in cases and vaults in dozens of museums and labs. The Remarkable Fraternity, frozen at twenty-four men, pruned now to twenty, are remembered—by deed, if not always by name—for what they accomplished, and are honored—by historians, if not always by the public—as the anniversaries of those missions come and go. Hardly a month passes when, in some small but significant way, someone does not acknowledge the astonishing accomplishments of the nine manned missions the United States launched to the moon.

Or of eight of them anyway. On April 11, 1970, at 1:13 P.M. Houston time—13:13 military time—Apollo 13, NASA's fifth lunar mission and its third planned landing, was launched with commander Jim Lovell and crew-mates Jack Swigert and Fred Haise aboard. Two days later, on April 13, when the crew was nearly five-sixths of the way to the moon, a two-foot tank of compressed liquid oxygen exploded like a bomb in the aft end of the spacecraft, irreparably crippling the ship and robbing the three astronauts of both power and breathable atmosphere nearly 200,000 miles from home. With barely minutes to spare before their cockpit went cold, dead, and airless, the crew abandoned ship and took refuge in their attached lunar lander, a frail, spindly ship with enough resources to keep two men alive for only two days. But there were now three men aboard and they were four days from home.

For the next eighty-seven hours, the world—which had already grown complacent over humanity's newly proven ability to take itself out to the moon—watched transfixed as Lovell, Swigert, Haise, and the space agency as a whole struggled to bring the crew home. The odds were long, the rescue improbable, and the crew, in some quarters, was given up for dead. But on April 17, at around midday Houston time, the spacecraft that circumstance had likely condemned to permanent drift in the icebox of space splashed down in the warm waters of the South Pacific, its pilots haggard and worn but undeniably alive.

The celebration that attended the return of Apollo 13 was a tumultuous one, and the three astronauts, who had left the planet with the kind of subdued send-off appropriate to the twelfth, thirteenth, and fourteenth men who would travel to the moon, returned to a reception more suited to the first, second, and third. There were parades and speeches, proclamations and medals, goodwill trips and handshake tours. And then, as suddenly as the reception began, it ended.

Apollo 13 had succeeded in bringing its imperiled crew home, but it had failed—the press and the public decided—in nearly every other way. Never mind that the astronauts themselves were not to blame for the explosion that ruined their ship. Never mind that the men in Mission Control were also blameless. Apollo 13 had been sent to the moon with a furled flag and empty sample-boxes and the explicit instructions to plant the flag in the lunar foothills and return with the boxes full of rocks. It had failed to carry out those instructions and thus, it was felt, it had failed. The crew of Apollo 13 would take their place in the Remarkable Fraternity with a loss of neither stature nor face, but the mission they flew would always be seen as a *lesser* mission, a black-mark mission, a stumble rather than a step in humanity's great lope to the stars.

For years, the history of the Apollo program and its fifth flight to the moon would be recorded just this way, and then, in 1992, all that began to change. Late that year, Jim Lovell decided to collaborate on a book that would at last tell the story of Apollo 13 as the dramatic tale of peril and triumph it was. The book would explain the mission, explain the hardware, explain the men behind the rescue. Most important, it would explain what Jim Lovell and every other test pilot who ever climbed into a spacecraft knew: that flying into orbit or out to the moon was, by its very nature, experimental flying, and experimental flying, by its very nature, entailed accidents. The standard by which you judged yourself was not how well you avoided such mishaps, but how you overcame them when they inevitably happened. When you understood that, you understood that Apollo 13 was an unparalleled success; and when you understood *that,* you knew Jim Lovell had an astounding tale to tell.

Not many people yet appreciated that fact, but Ron Howard—the director of such movies as *The Paper, Far and Away, Backdraft, Parenthood,* and

Splash—along with producer and partner Brian Grazer at Imagine Films, did. Early in 1993, Howard and Grazer learned of the Apollo 13 book, contacted the authors, and said that even before the manuscript was written, they would like to begin developing the story into a movie. For the better part of the following year, both book and screenplay sped toward completion—with Lovell lending his guidance to both—and in the spring of 1994, the Howard-Grazer film *Apollo 13,* starring Oscar winner Tom Hanks as Jim Lovell, as well as Kevin Bacon, Bill Paxton, Gary Sinise, Ed Harris, and Kathleen Quinlan, went into production.

Making the movie was a decidedly less hazardous business than flying the Apollo 13 mission, but it was no less labor intensive. Filming took place in three states, on dozens of sets and, for four remarkable weeks, at a point 36,000 feet in the air, inside the zero-gravity environment of a NASA KC-135 aircraft. Whole sound stages at Universal Studios in Los Angeles were chilled down to just above freezing to re-create the interior of the Apollo 13 spacecraft during the long, powerless coast back to Earth. With the aid of Max Ary of the Kansas Cosmosphere and Space Center, mock-ups of the interiors and exteriors of both the command module and lunar module were built and, with the aid of computer artists, those models and others were incorporated into the film. Consultants like Lovell, Apollo 15 commander Dave Scott, and Mission Control veterans Gerry Griffin and Jerry Bostick were brought in to ensure the technical accuracy of the screenplay, props, and set. The Imagine team spent more than a year preparing to make their movie, more than four months actually shooting it, and then another half year editing, refining, and folding in their remarkable special effects.

The Apollo Adventure is a dual chronicle, the story of the making of both the *Apollo 13* film and the entire Apollo program that inspired it. The cinematic half of the story is told through peeks behind the scenes at Universal, at Imagine, at the studios of Digital Domain, where the special effects were created, and even into the KC-135 weightlessness airplane. The Apollo part of the tale is the result of more than two years of research into the history of America's journeys to the moon and offers inside accounts of some of the lunar program's most controversial, most perilous, most intimate, and most triumphant moments. Also included are transcripts of once-secret recordings made inside the cockpits of the command and lunar modules as the astronauts left Earth, arrived at the moon, and landed on its surface. These recordings, never broadcast to Earth during the missions, were heard and transcribed only when the crews returned, after which they were stamped CLASSIFIED and locked away in NASA's vaults. Now they have been declassified.

The jobs of flying to the moon and making a film about one such mission seem, superficially, to have little in common, and the players involved in such a twin-venue tale—players with names like Lovell and Haise, Howard and Hanks, Armstrong and Paxton and Borman and Bacon and Harris and Scott and Sinise—at first seem to have even less in common. Nearly thirty years ago, however, thousands of Americans dedicated themselves to the ambitious goal of putting a handful of their countrymen on the surface of the moon; more than a generation later, an equally driven if somewhat smaller group dedicated themselves to telling the story of one of those missions in a way it had never been told before. The cost, the scope, and the life-and-death stakes of the two projects may have been different, but the commitment, drive, and fierce dedication to doing the job right were precisely the same. *The Apollo Adventure* tells both tales.

THE
APOLLO
ADVENTURE

The *Apollo 13* actors posing as astronauts posing for publicity shots in the days before the launch of the real Apollo 13.

1

Crucible

Joe Shea, so the rumors ran, kept the picture of the three crewmen hanging in his home. People were surprised by that—people were *more* than surprised by that—after what had happened and all. But Shea evidently saw nothing wrong with it.

It wasn't as if many people at the Agency had a chance to go over to Joe Shea's house and see for themselves if the picture was really hanging where everybody said it was. Someone in the rarefied position Shea held in the NASA hierarchy—chief of the Apollo program office—hardly had the time to have everyone who worked for him over for a social call. And even if you did wind up at a dinner party or a cocktail function at the Shea house, you couldn't exactly go looking for the thing.

Certainly, Shea wasn't alone in decorating his home with this kind of memento. There wasn't an Agency employee or contractor worth his NASA credentials who didn't have a few astronaut pictures of his own hanging in the den or the entrance foyer. Maybe you were working as floor foreman at North American Aviation in Downey, California, one afternoon when Wally

Schirra came out to the plant to check on the progress of his Apollo command module. At the end of the day, a photographer would be called in, the astronaut would pose with his arm around your shoulder, and by the end of the week, the picture would arrive with an inscription from Wally in which he called you by your first name—*always* your first name—thanked you for the work you were doing, and maybe even made some jokey tech-talk reference that only people like you and your coworkers and your friend the astronaut would understand. What you did with a picture like that was you showed it to your wife and you put it in a frame and you dusted off the glass and you hung it in your house and you made damn sure you picked a spot where nobody coming in your front door could fail to notice it.

All over Houston and Florida there were pictures like that—from Wally Schirra or Gordon Cooper or Frank Borman or Jim Lovell or Neil Armstrong or Pete Conrad or Deke Slayton or Tom Stafford or Dave Scott or Dick Gordon or plenty of others, and nobody raised any eyebrows when the owners of *those* pictures hung them up. Of course, Wally and Gordon and Frank and Jim and Neil and Pete and Deke and Tom and Dave and Dick and the others were still alive. Gus Grissom and Ed White and Roger Chaffee weren't. If the astronauts in *your* picture were dead—and if the people both inside and outside the Agency had always asked whether or not the people in your program were responsible—well, you might think twice about just how prominently you wanted to display that particular artifact.

It was August of 1966—August 19 actually, 161 days before the end of Gus Grissom's and Ed White's and Roger Chaffee's lives—when Joe Shea got his picture, and what people were talking about that day was the likelihood of someone dying in a spacecraft. Shea and Grissom were at a meeting at the North American Aviation plant discussing just how ready the brand-new three-man Apollo spacecraft was for its maiden voyage into space, now scheduled for just a few months away. As Apollo missions went, it wouldn't be much—an unglamorous workhorse flight into low Earth orbit during which Grissom and his junior crewmates, White and Chaffee, would be asked to do little more than test-drive the ship that would one day make far more exotic trips to the moon. But since this was the shakedown flight—the first time the Agency would ever try something as audacious as putting three men into space at once in an oversize vehicle with more habitable space than the family

The interior of the mock-up Apollo 13 command module.

station wagon—people were pretty excited. Since the ship seemed utterly incapable of making the trip, people were also pretty nervous.

In the months leading up to the planned launch of Apollo 1, Grissom, White, and Chaffee's craft—known simply as Spacecraft Number 012—had suffered countless technical breakdowns, including electrical problems, heat-shield problems, communications problems, environmental problems, engine and other problems. NASA, closing in fast on the deadline imposed by former president Kennedy's audacious promise to have men on the moon by the end of the decade, had been asking the North American Aviation company, the builders of the Apollo Command and Service Modules, ever more insistently if all these technical problems would ever be resolved, and North American had been promising ever less persuasively that they would. If the ship was ever going to lose its bloodless *012* designation, earn the honorific *Apollo 1,* and carry its crewmen into space sometime this winter, the corporate engineers would have to make good on that promise. Grissom and Shea were here today to see how they were coming.

Joining the astronaut and the project chief in the corporate conference room were other representatives of both NASA and North American, including Chris Kraft, the space agency's director of flight operations, Harrison Storms, the head of North American Aviation, and a number of other technicians and administrators from both groups. As soon as the men settled into their seats,

Shea called the gathering to order. From his first words, it was clear he was in no mood to dither.

"I hope the meeting moves . . . quickly," he said simply. "This is not a design meeting to bring up old bitches. It's a meeting specifically concerned with Spacecraft 012 and its suitability to leave the plant and begin the checkout procedures and booster-mating procedures down at the Cape. Noted in some of the earlier meetings associated with 12, we were getting ourselves all tangled up [in] design changes. . . . This meeting is not to talk about specific changes; it's to talk about the spacecraft as presently defined by North American and NASA."

If the intention of Shea's declaration was to limit the discussion, he could not have stated it terribly persuasively, because as soon as he relinquished the floor, a string of new problems and old bitches were immediately raised. There was the power failure in both main buses of the electrical system the previous morning. There were the wiring changes that still had to be performed in the spacecraft's service module. There were the troublesome leaks in the spacecraft suit loops. There were problems with the demand regulator and the water accumulator. There were spacecraft panels that had been removed and had not yet been reverified. Most important, a performance test had yet to be conducted on the spacecraft's heavy, triple-layer, vaultlike hatch. What would happen, some of the engineers worried, if there were an emergency of some kind on the launch pad and the crew had to escape—*egress,* as the flight planners liked to say—in a hurry? Would three scrambling astronauts be able to make it out in time through a door that was bolted in place with more than twenty locks and latches? Before the ship could be certified fit, a drill would have to be conducted to make sure such a lifesaving exit was possible.

The litany of technical issues droned on, with much of the discussion focusing on the environmental control system, or the ECS. Finally, Gus Grissom rose to speak. Grissom was known as a gruff, sober soul who brooked little nonsense when it came to the care and building of his spacecraft. On-site at Downey for much of Spacecraft 012's design and checkout work, he had grown increasingly dissatisfied with the condition of the ship he'd been asked to command and did not hesitate to report back to NASA when something displeased him. Today, though, a trace of whimsy was in Grissom's demeanor.

"I've got [some] things I'd like to mention right now," he began. "They really don't have to do with the ECS, I guess." Grissom turned his attention

The prime crew, in April 1966, of the doomed Apollo 1 mission. From left to right: Edward White II, Virgil "Gus" Grissom, and Roger Chaffee. *(NASA)*

away from the group at large and looked toward Storms. "Stormy occasionally gives us hell for calling back to Houston, so we've got a little memento here to remind him that we do occasionally talk to other people."

Grissom produced a glossy eight-by-ten photograph and passed it down to Storms. As the North American boss and the people around him looked at the picture the astronaut had produced, they erupted into laughter. Grissom, appreciating their reaction, began to laugh, too. In the picture, Gus Grissom, Ed White, and Roger Chaffee sat side by side in their zippered flight suits in the slightly stiff posture favored by astronauts posing for NASA promotional pictures. In front of them on a table was a tiny model of their Apollo 1 spacecraft. Behind them was an American flag. Rather than looking smilingly and confidently toward the camera as the typical crew would, however, Grissom, White, and Chaffee had their heads bowed over the model, their eyes closed, and their hands held prayerfully before them.

Stormy, the inscription read, *this time we are not calling Houston!*

From a man as grim as Gus could be, this was funny stuff. Grissom making a joke was unexpected enough. Grissom making a joke about the condition of his spacecraft was without precedent.

As the laughter was beginning to subside, Grissom announced, "Now, we've got one for Joe Shea also. He advised us to practice our backup procedures religiously, so here we are practicing."

The crowd laughed anew.

"I don't know how many of you saw this picture," Shea said to the engineers and executives elsewhere in the room as he took his picture from Gus, "but they are all in very pious attitudes. They had a lot of practice preying on the North American people."

After another few moments of appreciative laughter at the unexpected badinage between the astronaut and the administrators, the meeting resumed, and the string of problems with the suddenly less ominous seeming spacecraft continued. For the remainder of the meeting, these technical issues were duly addressed and discussed. Before the meeting ended, a few more moments of good-natured laughter would lead to more goodfellowship than the troubled spacecraft had generally produced.

One hundred and sixty-one days later, Gus Grissom, Ed White, and Roger Chaffee would climb inside Spacecraft 012 for a countdown dress rehearsal atop the Saturn 1-B booster that was to carry them into space. Within hours, they would burn to death as a flaw in the balky electrical system triggered a flash fire that claimed their lives well before they could hope to open their clamped and armored hatch. The men in the room at North American Aviation would deeply mourn the crew, the nation would bury them with full military honors, and Joe Shea would ultimately hang his inscribed picture inside the front door of his home in Weston, Massachusetts.

NASA engineers did not spook easily. Yes, there was always the possibility that the trio of pilots placed in your charge would never make it back to the ground alive; yes, there was the ever-present awareness that the missile you were preparing to launch today could find its way not into space, but into the heart of some nearby blameless city. But this was the risk you took—the risk the nation took—for toying with these big, ballistic machines in the first place. As long as you looked at things this way, you were impervious to worry—or impervious to *most* worries. But for all your resistance to rumination, one

Actress Kathleen Quinlan in the NASA VIP gallery at Mission Control.

The *Washington Post* the morning after the Apollo 1 fire.

thing did scare you, one thing frustrated even your best, most professional attempts at imperturbability: a fire in the spacecraft.

When NASA engineers were first designing the metal canisters in which their pilots would be flung into space, they required simplicity in all things. The more hardware you put in a ship, the more there is to crap out on you. Certainly you needed backup systems; certainly those backup systems needed backup systems. But once you had your main hardware and your redundancy hardware in place, everything else was expendable. Among the first things to be simplified in this battle to downsize was the atmospheric system.

Earthly air is composed of a whole soup of gases, including oxygen, nitrogen, carbon dioxide, methane, argon, and water vapor. It is the oxygen alone, however—which represents barely 20 percent of the mix—that is needed to sustain life, and so this gas alone would be sent aloft with the crew. Of course, oxygen sustains not only life, it also sustains fire—and *pure* oxygen

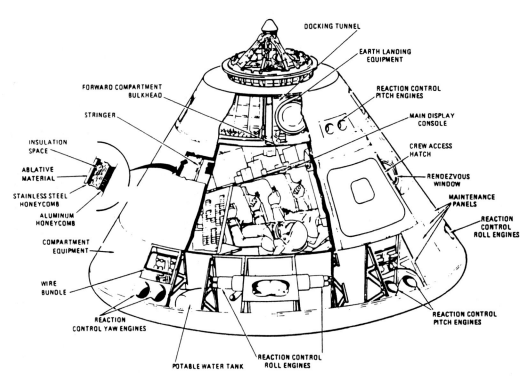

Command module. *(NASA)*

sustains it best of all. Fill a cockpit with pressurized O_2, strip away all the other, nonflammable gases that make the terrestrial atmosphere the sodden blanket it is, and it would take a single, stray spark for your multimillion-dollar spacecraft to become, in a flash, a multimillion-dollar warhead.

Both the astronauts and the engineers knew the risks of flying a ship with so explosive a pocket of air inside, and neither group was very comfortable with it. To help the pilots prepare for the unlikely but undeniable risk of an onboard conflagration, the designers did what designers do when faced with the seemingly uncontrollable: they tried to control it. In the case of space-agency flight planners, control meant writing mission rules. Astronauts climbing into a spacecraft carried with them loosely bound steno books filled with page upon page of potential mission catastrophes and methods for dealing with them. Suppose there was a pressure leak in the command module. Suppose the drogue chutes failed to open. Suppose the booster went wild, the

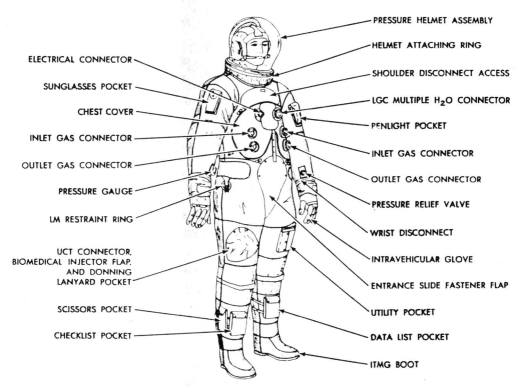

Pressure garment assembly. *(NASA)*

thrusters went south, the fuel cells went dead, the guidance went haywire. Each calamitous possibility was listed dispassionately in the steno books, along with a series of deliberate, easy-to-memorize steps detailing how that particular emergency should be addressed most effectively.

When it came to fire, the steps were simple. As soon as you catch your first whiff of fire, climb into your pressure garments, don your helmets, pressurize the suits, then instantly open your cabin vents, dumping the whole load of pressurized, flame-feeding cockpit atmosphere into surrounding space.

Among the problems with this straightforward plan, the gravest was that merely "climbing into" a pressure suit was not so simple a matter. The mission protocols listed forty-five separate steps needed to don a suit successfully, including unstowing helmets, uncapping nozzles, zippering boots, locking inlets, closing visors, and twist-locking gloves. The final step in the long list required that the commander "record on flight log donning times, problems encountered, and comments."

Even if suiting up had been a simpler matter, the fire procedures presented another, bigger problem. Any emergency protocol, especially a protocol as extreme as this one, would almost certainly spell the end of the mission. With a single lunar flight costing upward of $400 million, flight planners did not take such steps casually. In the Apollo *Operations Handbook* dated November 30, 1966—or two and a half months before the scheduled liftoff of Grissom, White, and Chaffee's flight—the cabin conditions or equipment malfunctions that would or wouldn't lead to a fire abort were specified.

"Cabin temp above 95°F," one malfunction on the list read.

"Continue mission," read the ruling next to it. "Turn off cabin fans."

"Smoke or annoying odors in suit," read another malfunction entry.

"Continue mission," repeated the ruling. "Open direct O_2 to purge suits."

"Smoke in cabin," persisted a third malfunction.

"Continue mission," the ruling repeated, then softened enough to add grudgingly, "Crew may elect to abort if source of smoke cannot be located and contained."

The wisdom of building a ship such as the one NASA had built and managing it with these kinds of protocols raised at least a few eyebrows within the aerospace industry and the Agency itself. But on November 30, 1966, when the book of mission techniques was issued and approved, the Apollo 1 crew was in the last stages of preparation for their planned flight into space, and nobody was inclined to rewrite the rules now. The protocols, they figured, were good; the safety precautions were adequate. Whether a crew strapped in place inside a vault-like cockpit that had suddenly begun to flame like an oven could ever actually "elect to abort" their mission, however, did not appear to occur to anyone.

Nobody noticed the little metal door on the little metal cabinet inside the Apollo 1 cockpit as it swung open and swung shut, just above the bundle of electrical cable than ran beneath it. Gus Grissom would reach inside to pull something from the cabinet and—*scrape*—the bottom of the door might shave a bit of insulation away. A moment later, he'd close the door again and—*scrape, scrape*—a bit more might be gone.

No one noticed either when the arc of electricity jumped from the newly bared wire, or some other undetected wire, striking nearby nylon netting, causing it to smolder. During the countdown dress rehearsal the crew was plodding through at 6:31 P.M. on the evening of January 27, 1967, mission rules called for all three astronauts to be wearing their helmets with the face plates closed. The fine curls of smoke that began rising from the netting were thus impossible for anyone in the ship to smell and, since they were still so tenuous, impossible to see as well. Even cockpit temperature sensors did not detect the tiny but building blaze, since, for a few seconds at least, the metal bulkhead of the spacecraft absorbed most of the heat.

As the nylon netting began to burn faster, a flicker of flame reached up and grazed a line of Velcro patches—used to secure loose equipment—affixed to the bulkhead. With its millions of whiskers of fabric and the generous wash of oxygen flowing through the strands, the Velcro would quickly begin to burn as well.

At this point Grissom, in his left-hand seat, Ed White, in the center, and Roger Chaffee, off to the right, would probably have noticed the crazy play of orange and white light coming from the lower reaches of their cockpit. No sooner would they have spotted the flickering fire than more Velcro, more netting, and now fabric cargo pouches would have begun to burn as well, carrying the fire up the spacecraft wall. It was probably at that moment—though no one knows for sure—that Roger Chaffee, the one rookie among the crew, called out, "Fire in the spacecraft!" alerting the ground crew to the sudden conflagration behind the triple-hulled hatch of the clamped and sealed ship.

In the time it took Chaffee to call out his warning, the astronauts—flat on their backs and restrained by straps in their metal and canvas couches—would have seen the sheet of fire complete its eyeblink climb up the wall and curve to the right, obscuring the ceiling and the instrument panel above their heads. With the panel mere inches from their faces, the fingers of flame would have been closer still, and this might have been what prompted White to call out the second alarm: "Fire in the cockpit!"

Gus Grissom, who said nothing, then did what the Apollo *Operations Handbook* said the commander should do and opened the cabin vent to dump the exploding atmosphere inside the cockpit into the warm, wet Florida atmosphere outside it. The problem was, while the vent switch was on Grissom's side of the cockpit, the vent itself was on the opposite side. The instant Grissom turned the crank, the compressed spacecraft atmosphere rushed to the right, carrying the fire—which was still largely confined to the left side of the ship—with it. The flame would now be covering the recumbent crew like a thick, killing quilt, and it was probably this, more than anything else, that caused Chaffee to issue the last reported alarm from the ship. "We've got a bad fire!" he called. "Let's get out! Open 'er up!"

The crew, of course, could not get out on their own, and with three layers of hatch steel and more than twenty latches separating the interior of the ship from the exterior, nobody on the gantry that surrounded the booster could do anything so simple as merely opening the ship up. Instead, the fire continued to feed on the oxygen left inside the cockpit, consuming cloth, netting, even metal, and causing the internal pressure to climb steadily and dangerously. When it had crested to twice the pressure of sea-level air, the aneurysm of heat and flame inside the ship finally burst open the craft, and in the floor to the right of Chaffee's couch, a gash suddenly appeared, through which the spacecraft at last hemorrhaged its flames into the air around it.

As soon as Apollo 1 ruptured, its internal inferno began to die, but many long minutes would pass before the pad crew at last wrestled open the hot, griddlelike door and peered inside.

The astronauts were dead. Nobody fighting to get into the ship realistically expected to find anything else. Nevertheless, the three men had been left surprisingly unmolested. There were the odd body burns, but these weren't enough to kill. Rather, the doctors would later conclude, the fumes released by the flames had done the real damage, filling with searing poisons the lungs of the men who just seconds before had been breathing only the purest oxygen.

It was just as well, of course, that the crew of Apollo 1 died so quickly. All of the newspapers would repeat that point. The heat inside the ship, it was ultimately revealed, had climbed above 1,400 degrees. The cabin thermometers, which were never supposed to record temperatures anywhere near that, couldn't register such a stratospheric figure, but the blackened interior—including a melted aluminum mass that had once been Gus Grissom's armrest—told the inferno-like tale. Indeed, by the time the armrest began to liquefy—barely twelve seconds after the fire began, if you believed the later estimates of flame propagation time—the crew was probably already gone. The newspapers repeated that, too, citing the twelve-second figure over and over and remarking repeatedly at the mercy of such a brief flash of suffering. It was not clear, of course, if any of the writers stopped to contemplate what those twelve short seconds felt like. If they did, they certainly didn't do so in print.

Ron Howard conferring with partner and producer Brian Grazer in the movie's Mission Control VIP gallery.

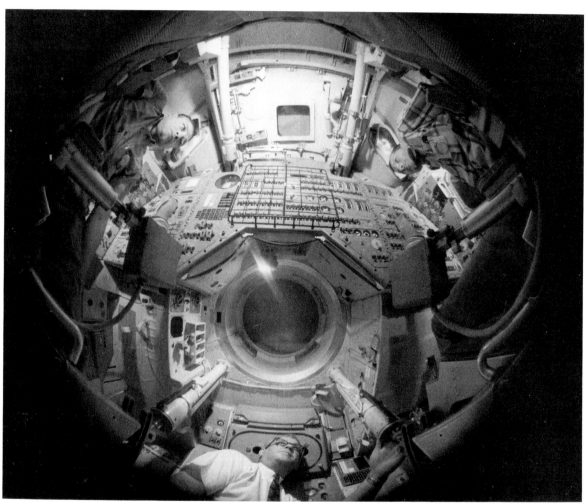

Just twenty-one months after the Apollo 1 fire, the command module had been redesigned, rebuilt, and readied for launch. *(NASA)*

NASA

2

The Contentious
Flight of Apollo 7

Betty Grissom, Gus's widow, got up just after sunrise on the morning of the first manned Apollo launch in 1968. It was a Friday in early October, and Fridays meant rousting her three sons out of bed, putting their breakfast on the table, and seeing that they left for school on time. Even if the Grissom boys didn't need their mother's help to stick to their morning schedule, however, Betty would probably have been up early. This Friday was a launch day in Houston, and for the insular NASA community encamped in the suburbs surrounding the Manned Spacecraft Center, launch days always began at the first suggestion of dawn. Even if your circadian clock—set and synchronized by the ambient tension when your husband or your friend or the husband of a friend was riding the tip of the rocket being launched that morning—didn't get you out of bed early, the roiling swarm of reporters and the rumbling fleet of TV trucks here to cover the event would.

Today, the newspeople weren't coming to Betty Grissom's house, of course; at one time they had, but no longer. However,

Kevin Bacon suited up prelaunch in the movie *Apollo 13*.

they were coming right next door. Next door was where Wally and Jo Schirra lived, and by seven o'clock—four hours and three minutes before the scheduled liftoff time—the fourth estate had already made itself at home on the Schirra estate. Most of the newsmen were respectful enough to keep their cameras and their eyes politely averted from the closed, quiet house next door, focusing instead on the buzzing, bustling home in front of them. It was here that Jo Schirra and eleven-year-old Suzanne were already stationed in front of their television set to watch as husband and father rocketed off Cape Canaveral's Pad 39 in command of the first American space mission in twenty-one months. Protocol and tradition limited the number—and even the gender—of the people who would be allowed inside the house, and with the exception of an occasional *Life* magazine photographer, it was usually a wives-only affair. Marge Slayton—wife of astronaut Deke Slayton—had spent the night and had gotten up early to make breakfast for the family. Annie Glenn, Louise Shepard, and Trudy Cooper—wives of John, Al, and Gordon—showed up shortly after. For the remainder of the day, these protective sentinels would be there to answer phones, make sandwiches, hold hands, and walk the Schirras through the thrilling, awful experience they had all lived so many times before.

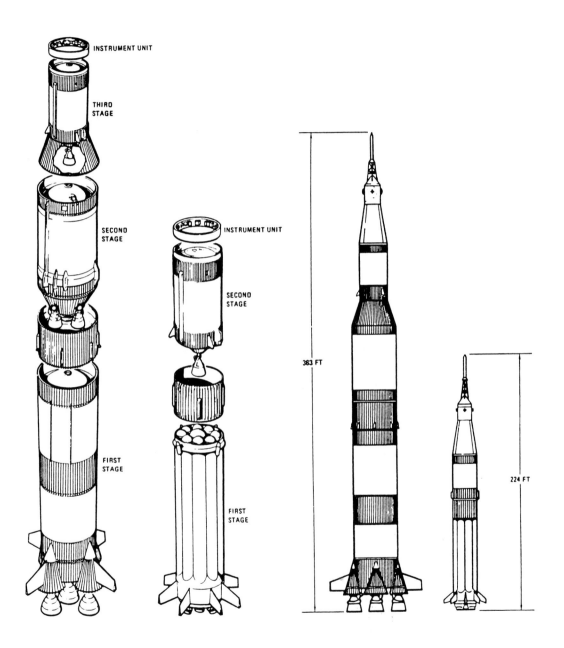

Saturn 5 (left) and Saturn 1-B. *(NASA)*

Of course, the Schirra house was not the only place the prelaunch drama was playing out. A few blocks away, a similarly jittery scene—with a similar coterie—was unfolding at the home of rookie pilot Donn Eisele, the man who would be riding the middle seat in the spacecraft today. Four states away, the largest crowd of all, made up of hundreds of media people and thousands of spectators—including Lo Cunningham, the wife of Walt Cunningham, the first-time pilot and the man assigned to the right-hand seat—had gathered around Cape Canaveral's knot of sandy spits and islands to watch first-hand as the bright white Saturn 1-B booster that was the focus of all the excitement today wrestled itself off the pad and into space. Whether the spacecraft was up to the job was nowhere near a sure thing.

As anyone involved in the day's launch would admit, the rocket itself was not much of a cause for concern—mostly because it just wasn't much of a rocket. In order to generate the thrust necessary to fling three men and their attendant hardware out to the moon, NASA needed a booster like none that had ever been built before. While the trusty Redstone rocket that had launched the first American into space in 1961 stood an impressive 82 feet from tail fin to tip, the new ship would have to measure more than 360 feet. While a fully fueled Atlas rocket like the one that had carried John Glenn into immortality in 1962 tipped the scales at a quarter of a million pounds, the new rocket would weigh over 6 million. While the Titan missiles that had successfully placed ten two-man Gemini spacecraft into Earth orbit from 1965 to 1966 generated an impressive 400,000 pounds of thrust, the imagined moon booster would have to roar from the pad with something like 7.5 million. Designed by German rocket builder Wernher von Braun, the mammoth machine was part of a new series of boosters known as the Saturns—a fifth-generation member of that remarkable family dubbed, appropriately, the Saturn 5. By even the most skeptical estimates, the Saturn 5 was a magnificent ship; but to date, it was also an unproven ship.

Happily for Wally Schirra, Donn Eisele, and Walt Cunningham, the rocket they would be riding this morning was not the big, experimental Saturn 5. With today's mission intended to be little more than an eleven-day shakedown cruise of the three-man Apollo spacecraft in low Earth orbit, thirty-six stories of rocket and 7.5 million pounds of oomph would have been far more missile than was necessary. Instead, the crew would be carried into space atop the Saturn 5's lesser brother, the Saturn 1-B. Standing 224 feet tall, the Saturn 1-B was a comparatively humble two-stage affair whose first stage consisted of

The prime crew, in May 1968, of the first manned Apollo space mission, Apollo 7. From left to right: Donn Eisele, command module pilot; Walter Schirra Jr., commander; and Walter Cunningham, lunar module pilot. *(NASA)*

eight little Redstone engines bundled together. Generating barely 1.6 million pounds of thrust, the Saturn 1-B was a popgun compared to the Saturn 5, but what the little booster had all over its bigger sibling was that it was reliable. The Redstone engine, the astronauts knew, was one of the sturdiest ever built, and a crew heading for an eleven-day journey in space could do a lot worse than to begin their trip with a ride atop eight of the trusty dynamos.

But if the Saturn 1-B rocket that would carry Schirra, Eisele, and Cunningham into orbit inspired confidence, the Apollo spacecraft that would be their home while they were there inspired something else entirely.

For months before the deaths of Grissom, White, and Chaffee on that January night in 1967, the astronauts had worried that NASA and North American Aviation were building a disastrous ship. The astronauts had been proven right in the most horrific of ways, and the spacecraft was eventually redesigned essentially to their specifications. Virtually all of the crewmen had had a voice in rebuilding the Apollo command module, but Schirra—as the man who had been Grissom's backup commander for the first Apollo flight and now, with his friend's death, had moved up to the starting team—had had one of the loudest voices of all. Flying regularly between NASA headquarters in

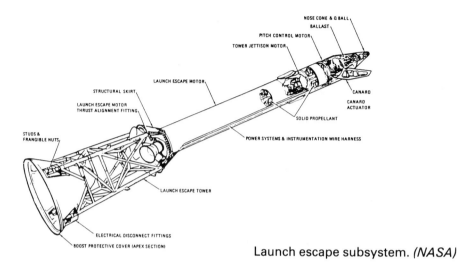

NOSE CONE & Q BALL
BALLAST
PITCH CONTROL MOTOR
TOWER JETTISON MOTOR
LAUNCH ESCAPE MOTOR
STRUCTURAL SKIRT
LAUNCH ESCAPE MOTOR THRUST ALIGNMENT FITTING
CANARD
CANARD ACTUATOR
SOLID PROPELLANT
STUDS & FRANGIBLE NUTS
POWER SYSTEMS & INSTRUMENTATION WIRE HARNESS
LAUNCH ESCAPE TOWER
ELECTRICAL DISCONNECT FITTINGS
BOOST PROTECTIVE COVER (APEX SECTION)

Launch escape subsystem. *(NASA)*

Houston and the spacecraft factory in California, Schirra made it his business to monitor every step of the redesign and to object—explicitly—when something was not to his liking. Usually those objections took him directly to the office of Harrison Storms, the North American Aviation chief.

"You guys want to fix this ship or not?" the astronaut liked to challenge the executive. "If so, let me see you down on the factory floor with the rest of us."

When the spacecraft was finally assembled to the astronauts' satisfaction, Schirra helped nursemaid it across the country and then pesonally sought to protect it from the prying eyes and wrenches of the Cape Canaveral technicians, who liked to check out a new ship themselves before validating it for launch.

"North American put this spacecraft together," he would say, now defending the corporate engineers he had spent so many months scrutinizing, "and I don't want you people taking it apart. It isn't your toy."

During this period, Schirra was regarded as either a highly professional, extraordinarily motivated, driven-to-excellence pilot—or as an enormous pain in the ass. The difference depended on whether it was yours or someone else's back he was riding that day. When the ship was at last built, checked out, and ceremonially christened Apollo 7—an homage to the lost crew of Apollo 1 and the five other unmanned flights that had flown before and since—most NASA folks believed that everyone would relax a bit.

The prime crew of the first manned Apollo space mission inside their spacecraft in December 1966. *(NASA)*

The Apollo command/service modules being mated with the Saturn 1-B booster in August 1968. *(NASA)*

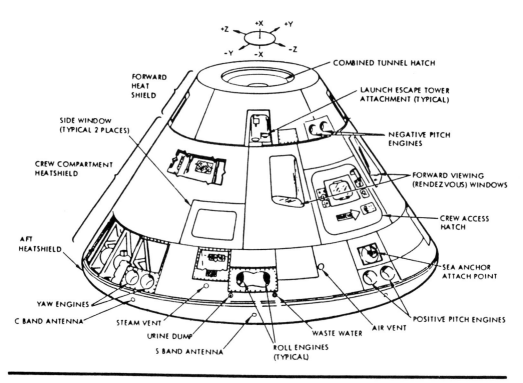

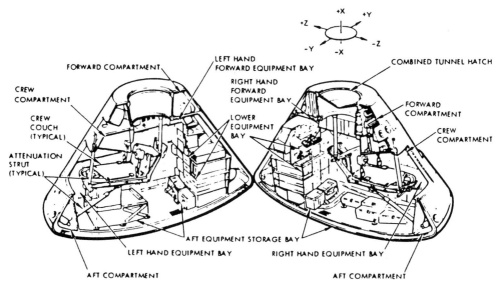

Command module. *(NASA)*

The ignition of the Apollo 7 rocket on October 11, 1968, took place as scheduled at 11:03 A.M., and it was immediately clear to the astronauts that they were riding a Cadillac of a booster. Schirra, who had had to endure the rocky liftoffs and the plastering g forces of both the Gemini-Titan and Mercury-Atlas rockets, was enthralled with this new breed of launch vehicle. It may not have been the magnificent Saturn 5, but the gentle climb and the almost nonexistent g load more than made up for that.

"She looks real good," the commander called down just under four minutes into the flight, as if evaluating a roadster he was considering taking home. "A little bumpy ride on this stage, but very pleasant."

Seconds before that call, at three minutes and twenty-one seconds into the flight, when the booster had carried the crew more than fifty miles up, the boost protective cover, or BPC, shielding the spacecraft from the atmospheric stresses of liftoff had been jettisoned, exposing the windows for the first time and revealing to the pilots the blackness they were climbing toward and the blue-green planet they were leaving behind. Now, after Wally's general endorsement of the soundness of the missile, his junior crewmates began voicing their approval of something much less technical, if much more pleasing: the scenery.

"This center-window view is sensational!" rookie Eisele shouted down over the roar of the engines.

"You finally got to look after the BPC went?" the capcom asked.

"Man, that was real fine," Eisele responded rapturously, only half-answering. "You'd think they raised a whole circus tent in front of us."

Ten minutes and forty-six seconds after leaving the sandy land of Cape Canaveral, Florida, Apollo 7 settled into a planned egg-shaped orbit above the Earth with a perigee, or low point, of 140 miles, and an apogee of 183 miles. There, they would scream along at 17,500 miles per hour, circling the planet once every eighty-nine minutes.

"Not bad shooting," the capcom complimented everyone concerned.

"That's great," a voice from the spacecraft agreed.

The air-to-ground goodwill lasted less than twenty-four hours. During the first day of the mission, a problem developed that can be routine to the point of being ignored on Earth, but can be murder in a sealed, pressurized cabin in which three men are living shoulder-to-shoulder twenty-four hours a day: someone developed a cold. In this case, it was the commander, and it soon

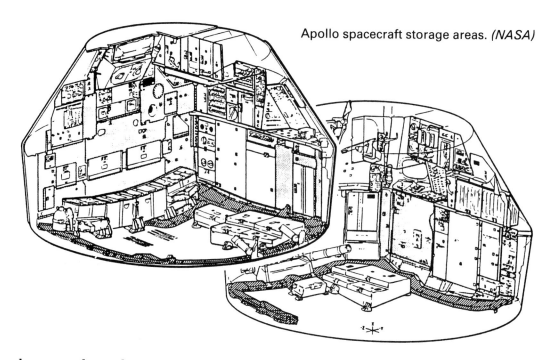

Apollo spacecraft storage areas. *(NASA)*

became clear that while a healthy Wally Schirra could be ornery, Wally Schirra with blocked ears, a congested head, and an utterly unproven spacecraft on his hands could be downright impossible. During the twenty-third hour of the mission, as the spacecraft was entering its sixteenth orbit, Houston had scheduled a television show that was to be broadcast live from space and beamed to networks and local affiliates across the United States. For an Agency still reeling from the catastrophe of early 1967, the TV show was an absolute must, intended to reassure taxpayers that NASA indeed had its $24 billion house in order and that America's moon program was running smoothly once again.

Schirra, however, who had earned his orbital wings in the days when astronauts went up alone, took whatever pictures they had time to take, and then carried them back to a NASA photo lab that was grateful to get its hands on whatever it could, had no time for such public affairs folderol. During the sixteenth orbit in which NASA flight planners expected the Apollo 7 crew to be making chat-show small talk with viewers at home, the commander was also supposed to prepare for a rendezvous exercise with the Saturn's spent second stage, which was floating in a nearby orbit. It was this maneuver that would be taking up his time, not a lot of smiling and waving at a TV camera.

"We had a flight plan update for TV," Schirra informed the ground at twenty-two hours and thirty minutes into the mission, "and will be unable to support anything but the normally scheduled flight-plan activities until after the rendezvous."

"Roger, understand," Bill Pogue, the capcom, responded uncertainly. ". . . We would just ask to reconsider that. It is in there at this particular time because of the passage over the [tracking] site."

"Roger, Bill, I understand," Schirra answered, unmoved. "We're going to be pretty busy along about then, and I think we're going to continue with what we had planned for normal activities."

Pogue was nonplussed. As the only people during a flight who were ever supposed to speak directly with the crew, the capcoms were trained to deal with all manner of technical, logistical, and scheduling problems. What they were less trained to deal with were personnel problems. The equipment aboard a spacecraft could always go balky on you, but the crewmen—drilled to within an inch of their sanity in the rules and procedures of space flight—were never supposed to be difficult. What's more, *this* crewman was Wally Schirra. Pogue, like all capcoms, was an astronaut himself, but he was an astronaut who had yet to make even his first trip into space. Schirra, now on his third orbital ride, was one of NASA's most senior pilots. The rookie would publicly cross the veteran only at his own peril.

"Roger," Pogue said respectfully, angling for time, "let me go over my TV update again there." Pogue allowed a second or so to elapse during which he gave his flight plan a cursory glance he didn't really need, then returned to the mike. "That time was twenty-three hours and fifty-three minutes, and it's possible I sent up the wrong time. Looks like at that particular time it could possibly be worked in."

"Roger," Schirra responded, probably knowing, like Pogue, that twenty-three hours and fifty-three minutes was *exactly* the time the capcom had sent up earlier. "No TV till after the rendezvous."

What any capcom could do to infuence such a willful commander was limited. One row farther back in Mission Control, however, was the console of the flight director, and his powers were considerably more sweeping. During a mission, the flight director's authority was *absolute* authority, and nothing that went out through the capcom's line and up to the ship went out without at least his implied imprimatur.

The flight director on duty at the moment was Glynn Lunney, a longtime

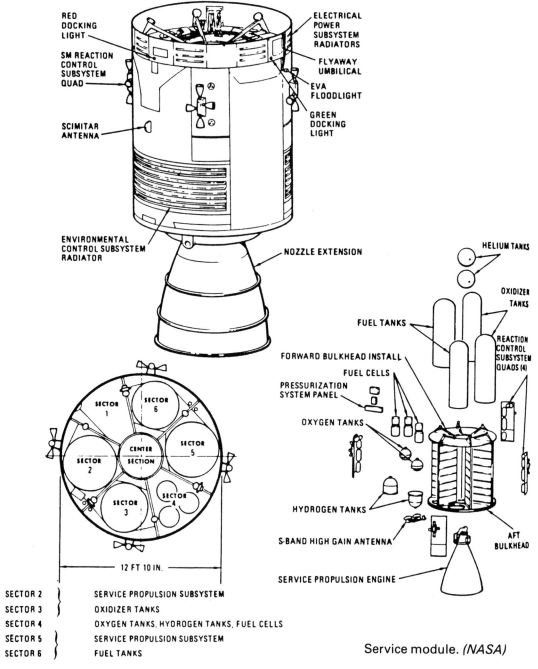

RED DOCKING LIGHT

SM REACTION CONTROL SUBSYSTEM QUAD

SCIMITAR ANTENNA

ENVIRONMENTAL CONTROL SUBSYSTEM RADIATOR

ELECTRICAL POWER SUBSYSTEM RADIATORS

FLYAWAY UMBILICAL

EVA FLOODLIGHT

GREEN DOCKING LIGHT

NOZZLE EXTENSION

HELIUM TANKS

OXIDIZER TANKS

FUEL TANKS

REACTION CONTROL SUBSYSTEM QUADS (4)

FORWARD BULKHEAD INSTALL

FUEL CELLS

PRESSURIZATION SYSTEM PANEL

OXYGEN TANKS

HYDROGEN TANKS

S-BAND HIGH GAIN ANTENNA

SERVICE PROPULSION ENGINE

AFT BULKHEAD

SECTOR 1
SECTOR 6
SECTOR 5
CENTER SECTION
SECTOR 2
SECTOR 3
SECTOR 4

— 12 FT 10 IN. —

SECTOR 2 } SERVICE PROPULSION SUBSYSTEM

SECTOR 3 } OXIDIZER TANKS

SECTOR 4 OXYGEN TANKS, HYDROGEN TANKS, FUEL CELLS

SECTOR 5 } SERVICE PROPULSION SUBSYSTEM

SECTOR 6 } FUEL TANKS

CENTER SECTION - SERVICE PROPULSION ENGINE AND HELIUM TANKS

Service module. *(NASA)*

veteran of these missions, and one who was inclined to brook little nonsense from his crews. Lunney dialed up Pogue on a private channel, told the capcom that the mission schedule was designed the way it was for a reason, that it would be followed as written, and that he, Pogue, would inform the crew as much. Pogue, serving two equally forbidding masters but realizing, wisely, that one was four feet behind him and the other was 183 miles above his head, went back on the air.

"Concerning the matter of television," he began, "there's been considerable discussion here in the center. The flight director wants you to turn on the television at the appropriate time."

Schirra seemed to accept this and spent the next few minutes reviewing navigational coordinates. Then, however, he clicked back on the air, as unmovable as ever. "You've added two burns to this flight schedule," he began, "and you've added a water dump, and we have a new vehicle up here, and I can tell you at this point that TV will be delayed without any further discussion until after the rendezvous."

A short time after that transmission, a public affairs officer was sent out to bring the media a simple message: Due to the complexity of the upcoming rendezvous and the numerous chores the crew still had to complete to prepare for it, it had been decided that the first television broadcast would be indefinitely postponed. Just who had done the deciding was not specifically discussed.

Within a day of the imbroglio over the television broadcast, the mood aboard Apollo 7 grew even worse. The crew compartment of an Apollo spacecraft measured 210 cubic feet—about the same habitable space found in an ordinary station wagon—and was maintained at a warm, humidified seventy degrees. The internal atmosphere was circulated through filters, but only at the glacial rate of 1.3 pounds every hour. Unless an extravehicular activity, or spacewalk, was scheduled—and there was none planned for Apollo 7—the hatch of the spacecraft would never be opened, meaning that the oxygen would never be dumped and the temperature would never change. A warm, wet, close environment like this is a virtual petri dish for viruses, and when one person falls ill in such an enclosure, it is all but certain that everyone else will as well. Before long, Wally Schirra's cold had spread to his crewmates—and so had his crankiness. Several days into the flight, an evaporator necessary for the recirculation of spacecraft water threatened to break down, and the capcom called up with a repair protocol that the controllers had helpfully devised. The man in the right-hand seat of the ship typically looked after all environmental matters, meaning that this particular maintenance job would fall to Walt Cunningham.

"Walt, we've been doing some discussion down here on a possible reservicing for the secondary evaporator," the voice from Earth announced good-naturedly, "and have come up with a procedure if you want to copy it."

"Is this something that somebody's dreamed up after all these months?" Cunningham said far less pleasantly. "I've been told that you can't reservice a secondary evaporator."

"That is correct, but we've come up with a procedure to do it."

"I don't know how everybody gets so smart in one week's time, but I'll go ahead and copy it. How long is it?"

"Oh, four steps."

"Very long steps?" the pilot asked long-sufferingly.

"No, real short."

"Okay, hit me with it. . . . But I'd just like to go on record as saying that people who dream up procedures like this only after you lift off have somehow been dropping the ball for the last three years. It looks kind of Mickey Mouse to me, but I'll stand by to do it if I have to."

Shortly afterward, Donn Eisele, who had so far held his tongue, got in on the feud with Mission Control when one of the biomedical sensors that had been attached to his chest before launch and was supposed to stay put until splashdown began to grow warm. Rather than discussing the problem with the ground, the rookie crewman simply elected to peel the electrodes off and stash them away. On the flight surgeon's monitor in Mission Control, the phosphorescent scribbles that had been tracking the astronaut's vital functions since before launch suddenly went flat-line. Before the doctor could sign on to the communications loop to inform the flight director of the problem, Eisele himself called down from the ship.

"I've got a little problem with my biomed," he announced casually. "One of the signal conditioners was getting quite hot, so I took the whole rig off and stowed it."

"Roger," the capcom responded. "Which one got hot? The black one or the blue one?"

"I don't know much about them. The one on the right."

"The one farthest right is the power supply."

"I don't care which one it is. I'm not going to wear it anymore."

For a media accustomed to the uninflected techno-patter of most space flights, such testiness from all three members of the Apollo 7 crew could not go unnoticed. Within a day, newspapers and wire services were filled with stories remarking on the "snappishness" of the crew, the "heavy-handedness" of their transmissions, the tendency of the veteran commander to "blow up" at small provocations. Even the Soviet Union, which had long monitored American space flights but reported on them only grudgingly, gave this flight a lot of play.

"Experts note," the Soviet wire services reported, "that the astronauts are showing increased irritation due to the monotony of their flight and the imperfect design of the systems for controlling the vital functions of the spacemen."

The NASA bosses in Houston were less than pleased with all this—and Chris Kraft was least pleased of all. Having served as flight director for all sixteen flights in the Mercury and Gemini programs, Kraft had striven for an almost military discipline from his crews. At the outset of the Apollo program, he had at last left his flight director's post, moving upstairs into NASA management where he could oversee the Apollo program as a whole. Notwithstanding, Kraft maintained a console in Mission Control from which he could continue to monitor his astronauts and his missions. Now, he did not like what he saw.

A flight director without portfolio had few options in a case like this. Signing on to the air to talk to the crew directly was not only a breach of protocol, but could also be interpreted as a direct challenge to the rotating team of successor flight directors who would be running this and subsequent Apollo missions. Doing nothing, however, and allowing the situation to deteriorate was not an attractive choice either. Happily, Kraft had a third alternative—in the person of Deke Slayton. As one of Wally Schirra's brethren in the original corps of Mercury astronauts, Slayton had perhaps more influence than anyone else in the Agency over the recalcitrant commander. As current head of the Flight Crew Operations Office—and thus the overseer of all the astronauts—he had even more influence over Wally's junior crewmen. If Slayton would spend a few minutes on the communications loop and try to talk some sense to the Apollo 7 crew, all of the air-to-ground animosity could at last be put to rest. The morning after the Eisele scrap, Kraft was considering asking Slayton to do just that, but as the former flight director walked into Mission Control, he found out that Deke had beaten him to it.

"You should know," Slayton said, intercepting Kraft before he could even make it to his console, "that last night I went on the line and had a talk with Wally." Kraft nodded. "I told him that the whole world was following this mission and that he and his crew were not coming across well."

"Good," Kraft said.

"I told him he was up there to do a job—"

Kraft nodded.

"—that he was *trained* to do a job—"

Kraft nodded.

"—and that he better get busy doing it."

"And? Kraft asked expectantly.

Slayton shrugged. "And he told me to go to hell."

The failure of the Apollo 7 crew to take Slayton's high-level scolding to heart was immediately evident. If Schirra, Cunningham, and Eisele had been testy during the first week of their mission, they were *extremely* testy during the second. On the crew's eighth day in orbit, the flight plan called for another much dreaded TV broadcast. This one actually went off on time, but when it was over, the crew found cause to complain about both the script they were required to follow during the program and the timing of the broadcast, which cut an hour out of their sleep schedule.

"Next time," Schirra growled to his capcom after the camera was turned off, "we'll have to get better material or better writers."

"It's also suggested better actors," the capcom muttered back, his own nerves beginning to fray.

"Actors Equity demands more sleep next time," Schirra retorted.

On the ninth day, when a navigation-test exercise did not work as planned, Wally actually became insulting. "I wish you would find out the idiot's name who thought up this test," he said. "I want to talk to him personally when I get down."

"While you're at it," Eisele chimed in, "find out who dreamed up the horizon test, too. That was another beauty."

Finally, as the crew was preparing for reentry, Schirra elected to break mission rules and allow himself and his crew to return to Earth with their pressure suits unpressurized and their helmets off, for fear that the atmosphere in the sealed suits would damage their cold-clogged ears. Slayton and Lunney, now concerned more with the crew's safety than with preserving their authority, implored Wally to change his mind, but the commander was unmoved.

"I guess you better be prepared to discuss in some detail when you land why you haven't got [the helmets] on," Slayton said in a final, futile transmission to the ship. "But it's your neck, and I hope you don't break it."

"Thank you, babe," Schirra answered airily. . . . "I'll be prepared to talk about the whole mission when we get back."

On October 22 at 7:11 A.M., Apollo 7 and its helmetless astronauts splashed down in the Atlantic, 325 miles south of Bermuda.

To hear NASA tell it, the flight had been an unalloyed success. To hear the astronauts tell it, they couldn't have been happier with the support they got from the fine men at the consoles in Mission Control. For reporters paying

The prime crew of Apollo 7 practice splashdown and egress techniques in the Gulf of Mexico in August 1968. *(NASA)*

attention to the air-to-ground small talk shortly before the end of the flight, however, it was clear that Deke Slayton, at least, was feeling a little less charitable than that.

"Hey, Deke," a tired and unshaven Cunningham called down to Earth in anticipation of the impeding splashdown, "I hope somebody meets us with a safety razor on that carrier."

"Roger," Slayton said simply but meaningfully. "I think there might be a couple."

Chris Kraft is not shy about showing off his "I Love Me" room. Kraft did not name it that, of course; his wife, Betty Anne, did. But Kraft himself adopted the term willingly, if abashedly.

Actually, you couldn't come up with a better name for the little den on the first floor of the Kraft home in suburban Houston. Decorated modestly and furnished unassumingly, it is filled with treasures and relics, artifacts and keepsakes, from Kraft's remarkable career in a remarkable program. There are photos with astronauts and letters from dignitaries; souvenir flags that flew into orbit and souvenir coins that flew to the moon; plaques presented to Kraft, newspaper stories about Kraft, and even the August 27, 1965, *Time* magazine cover, featuring a stylized painting of a much younger Kraft, looking out across the Mission Control auditorium that was once his to command.

Chris Kraft does not command missions into space anymore. Now and again he still makes the fifteen-minute ride over to NASA to advise and consult. But the pace he maintains is slower and the hours he keeps less killing. If the years haven't subdued Chris Kraft, they have softened his edges a bit. And one of the things he's softened most about is the contentious men of Apollo 7.

In the days that followed the splashdown of that most quarrelsome crew, forgiveness was the last thing on the former flight director's mind. Only hours after the spacecraft hit the water, the freshly showered, freshly shaven crew, dressed in crisp new coveralls, walked into the debriefing room to begin the exhaustive mission review that followed every flight. Waiting for them were doctors, engineers, and flight planners—as well as assistant administrator Christopher Kraft. Wally Schirra, his customary playful smile wavering a bit, faced his Agency superior.

"I wasn't sure you'd ever talk to me again," he said with uncharacteristic humility.

"I'm not sure I ever will," Kraft answered honestly.

Kraft's fury with his veteran commander was genuine, but as one of the men in the Agency planning office who determined upcoming missions and the crews that would fly them, he had a far more powerful weapon to wield than angry silence. Wally Schirra, Donn Eisele, and Walt Cunningham, Kraft decided, were through as astronauts. In the case of Wally Schirra, Kraft knew, this did not mean much. The three-time space pilot had made it clear before Apollo 7 that he would be leaving the astronaut corps after this mission and rejoining the private sector. A formal grounding, while still a powerful symbol, would therefore have no real effect on him.

Eisele and Cunningham, however, were a different matter. As first-time crewmen, they had other ambitions—*lunar* ambitions—and given that they had just been given the privilege to fly abroad the very first manned Apollo spacecraft ever to take to space, they were well on their way. Now, Kraft decided, they would be going nowhere. Too many other pilots, hungry for a mission, had never complained about a flight plan or barked at a capcom to reward these two with another chance. Even if Eisele and Cunningham never appreciated that what they did was wrong, perhaps astronauts on future missions would remember the two grounded pilots and think twice before they followed their example.

Kraft, of course, did not make this NASA equivalent of a death sentence public; it was simply assumed that when the time came to fill out crew manifests for future flights, the names of the Apollo 7 astronauts would always be left off. Outside official circles, however, Kraft could not always hold his tongue, and ultimately word got back to Walt Cunningham.

"Is it true," the astronaut asked one day in a call to the administrator, "that you've been telling people that the only way I'll fly again is over your dead body?"

Cunningham's forthright question elicited an equally forthright answer. "You got it right from the horse's mouth," Kraft said.

Chris Kraft was as good as his word, and though Donn Eisele and Walt Cunningham remained part of the astronaut corps after Schirra left, neither one would ever ride a rocket into space again. In the twenty-seven years since the flight of Apollo 7, Kraft has never regretted that decision, nor has he ever forgiven the behavior that led him to it. But now, a generation after the end of the Apollo program, sitting amidst the trophies in his I Love Me room, he at least understands it.

The Apollo 7 crew arriving aboard the USS *Essex,* the prime recovery ship for the 10.8-day Earth-orbital mission. The Apollo 7 spacecraft splashed down at 7:11 A.M. EDT, October 22, 1968, approximately two hundred nautical miles SSW of Bermuda in the Atlantic. *(NASA)*

"If you asked me at the time why Wally behaved the way he did," Kraft says, "I'd have said it's because he was a son of a bitch—in fact I probably *did* say that. But Wally wasn't a son of a bitch. He was an astronaut commanding a spacecraft that less than two years earlier had killed three men. Test pilots live with death all the time, and I don't think Wally was unduly shaken by this one. But that doesn't mean he wasn't affected by it—or that he didn't have a right to be. We were all ticked off at Wally at the time, but this was a man who had just watched three of his friends die. Thinking back on it, I can't say I blame him a bit."

Moscow: TASS International Service in English; 20:46 GMT; 15 Oct. 68

APOLLO-7 CHANGES FLIGHT, CHANGES ORBIT

New York—The American spaceship Apollo-7 continues its flight. Last night it made a maneuver to reduce the perigee of the ship's orbit. The new orbit has a perigee of 167 kilometers and an apogee of 269 kilometers.

Reporting on the health of the cosmonauts, agencies stress that Walter Schirra's flu worsened, while Walter Cunningham and Donn Eisele stopped complaining of dry mucous membrane.

Moscow: TASS International Service in English; 23:06 GMT; 15 Oct. 68

NEGRO-POLICE CLASHES CONTINUE IN WASHINGTON

Washington—Bitter clashes of Negroes with police, uncorked last week, continue unabated in the American capital. The new outburst of racial disturbances in Washington was sparked off by the wild and senseless killing by a white policeman of a Negro who crossed the street when the light was red. Several score Negro youths were taken to police stations. A curfew has been imposed on Negro youths in the city.

Moscow: TASS International Service in English; 15:03 GMT; 22 Oct. 68

APOLLO-7 CREW COMPLETES SUCCESSFUL MISSION

New York—At 14:12 Moscow time today, the U.S. Apollo-spacecraft carrying the three astronauts on board splashed down in the Atlantic. News agency reports say that the crew of three—Walter Schirra, 45, commander, Donn Eisele, 38, and Walter Cunningham, 36—after an 11-day strenuous space mission looked tired but extremely happy. Summing up the preliminary results of the mission, NASA spokesmen described it as rather successful. They note that the equipment on board the craft functioned normally in the main, even though the crew expressed certain displeasure with the helmets, some of the household and hygienic appliances, as well as the not always rational alternation of sleep, work, and meals.

Ron Howard (center) with his astronauts. From left to right: Kevin Bacon, Gary Sinise, Bill Paxton, and Tom Hanks.

3

Rehearsal for
the Moon

1969, APOLLO 11

It was tough to kill Neil Armstrong. Actually, judging by his
flight history, it was close to *impossible* to kill Neil Armstrong. Armstrong wouldn't admit it, of course; the last thing
any test pilot would do was challenge fate and fortune and his
good luck by suggesting that he was impervious to harm. But if
any pilot actually was indestructible, it just might have been
Armstrong.

It wasn't as if Neil Armstrong's equipment didn't *try* to kill
him. No astronaut seemed to be laboring under more of a hardware vendetta than the man who would one day be the first to
set foot on the moon. In the spring of 1966, Armstrong flew into
space in command of Gemini 8, an earth orbit mission that would
have been one of NASA's most ambitious efforts since the first
manned mission, a ballistic suborbital piloted by Al Shepard five
years earlier. Barely six hours after launch, however, a stuck
thruster caused his ship to begin spinning at a blackout-inducing
500 rpms, requiring the commander to abort his mission, fire his
retro-rockets, and plop down ignominiously in the first ocean that

rotated into position beneath his craft. Three years later, as commander of Apollo 11, Armstrong found himself hovering over a Sea of Tranquillity boulder field, looking for a clear place to set down, when his guidance computer flashed an alarm telling him that it was overloaded and that he'd have to land on his own. Already dangerously low on fuel, Armstrong had no choice but to comply, picking his way through the surrounding rubble until he found a clear spot and settling into the lunar dust barely seconds before his engine quit on him altogether.

But it was neither in Earth orbit nor on the remote plains of the moon that Neil Armstrong came the closest to piloting grief. Rather, it was two hundred feet above the hardscrabble of Ellington Air Force Base in Houston, while training for his moon mission in a nine-foot, puddle-hopping simulator that was never intended to fly more than a thousand feet from home. In this ungainly craft, the man who would one day fly a quarter of a million miles to the moon would survive a crash that a lesser pilot would surely not have survived.

Training for a space mission—particularly a lunar mission—was always a nasty business. The problem wasn't that the vehicles intended for space flight were inherently more dangerous than those intended for terrestrial flight—though they may well have been; and it wasn't that the mission profiles posed greater risks than the pilots had ever faced before—though they probably did. Rather, it was that the very nature of space flight required the astronauts to do something no test pilot in his right mind would *dream* of doing: flying a ship on an authentic, full-up mission without first having flown it hundreds of times in practice. For a pilot learning the hair-raising business of landing an F2H Banshee on the deck of an aircraft carrier, the training would begin in a classroom, then proceed to the cockpit of a locked-down Banshee sitting in a hangar. From the hangar, the apprentice would progress to a circle over the airfield, then a longer flight over the surrounding country- side, then, finally, an actual flight from an actual carrier. By the time he was ready for the first operational mission, he could fly his jet with a confidence bordering on arrogance.

In the case of space travel, things weren't so easy. With a single Apollo command module costing $40 million, and a full-up lunar flight costing $400 million, it was hardly possible to build enough ships and launch enough missions to allow every pilot a few orbital training flights before undertaking the genuine job of flying to the moon. Instead, NASA had to rely on simulators.

For an organization with billions a year at its disposal, NASA might not have been able to afford all of the spaceships it wanted, but it could afford some world-class mock-ups. Perhaps the most impressive—and certainly the least perilous—of the counterfeit craft were the so-called fixed-base simulators at NASA's facilities in both Houston and Florida.

As the name of the equipment self-evidently implied, fixed-base simulators were re-creations of the actual Apollo spacecraft, anchored in place on the floor of the NASA facilities. What was less obvious was how remarkable those re-creations were. During the Apollo program, the men who would fly the new ships would actually be flying two ships: the aerodynamic command-service module, which would serve as mother ship and ferry, taking all three astronauts out to the moon and back home; and the insectile lunar lander, the fragile, four-legged ship that would carry two of the astronauts down to the lunar surface. In the crew-training buildings, both ships were simulated with remarkable faithfulness. An actual command module had an instrument panel with fourteen different subpanels containing more than five hundred lights, switches, indicators, and dials, and so the simulator's instrument panels did, too. The genuine ship had a computer, navigation hardware, and a multichannel communications system, and so the ersatz ship did, too. Inside the genuine ship were three canvas-and-aluminum couches, 210 cubic feet of habitable space, and a color scheme of mostly institutional green and gunmetal gray, and so the interior of the mock-up looked the same. In the lunar-module simulator, things were similarly authentic, with faithful re-creations of all of the environmental displays, thruster controls, navigation telescopes, engine throttles, battery readouts, fuel gauges, water recirculators, orbital maps, star charts, air filters, and even storage cabinets and crash bars.

Inside these make-believe craft, the crews were put through hundreds of hours of simulated flights, intended to prepare them for virtually any problem they might face on an authentic mission. The problems were dreamed up by a team of technicians known as simulation supervisors, or simsups, sitting at consoles outside the ships, and the nature of the crises the simsups would invent was limited only by their imaginations—with one significant exception. Astronauts were never to be thrown a problem for which there was no solution. It would do little for morale, the simsups were told, to conduct a simulation whose resolution was the loss of the craft and the death of its occupants. Outside of this dark scenario, however, the men at the consoles were permitted to do their best to trip up the crew, and trip them up they often did.

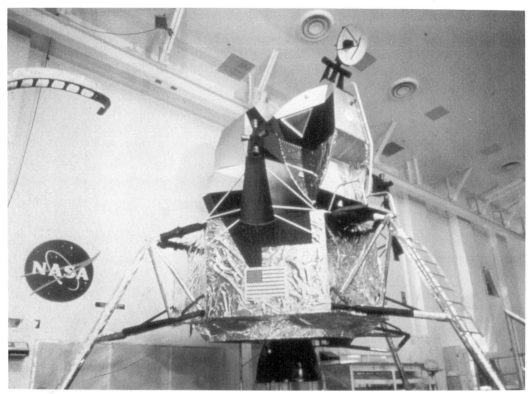

The lunar-module simulator in the movie.

Early in the training for the 1971 Apollo 15 mission, Dave Scott, a veteran of both Gemini 8 and Apollo 9, was running through a simulated liftoff with his rookie crewmates, Al Worden and Jim Irwin. During the make-believe burn of the Saturn 5's first stage, the simsups threw the crew a launch-abort problem, to test their ability to cope with a possible explosion in the mammoth first stage of their Saturn 5 booster seconds after liftoff. Scott, who had been through this drill countless times before, saw the problem coming but held his tongue to see if his first-timers could handle it. As it turned out, they couldn't, and the imaginary booster promptly augered into the Atlantic, taking all three men with it. A silence fell over the simulated spacecraft as it sank to its grave, and the simsups, pleased with their work, called for a short break. Scott, unruffled, climbed out of the ship and repaired to his office; a moment later, a shaken Irwin and Worden followed him there.

"I don't know what happened, Dave," Worden said, closing the door and sitting. "We just weren't fast enough."

"We're sorry," Irwin added. "They just got us."

Scott waved dismissively. "It's their *job* to get us. They write the scripts and from the moment you climb into that thing they're trying to bust your ass. I guarantee you, they're gonna kill us at least a few more times in that thing before we get to launch day."

As authentic as the simulations in the command module mock-up could be, the simulations in the lunar module were even more so. Since a pilot in a LEM (lunar excursion module) was always eyeballing the lunar surface and maneuvering toward a desired landing site, NASA designers decided that the windows on the simulated ship would not be windows at all, but triangular television screens. On the floor in a nearby room were gigantic relief maps of the lunar surface with television cameras suspended over them. As the commander of the LEM fired his thrusters this way and that and throttled his descent engine up and down, the cameras would move accordingly, bobbing and dipping and weaving and swooping, showing the two-man crew just what they would see as they maneuvered their ship around and over—and occasionally into—the terrain below.

During one goodwill tour of the Canaveral facilities in 1969, Apollo 8 command-module pilot and Apollo 13 commander Jim Lovell escorted French president Georges Pompidou into the simulator and delighted him with a simulated landing in a lunar crater. As the president and the astronaut descended toward their touchdown, Pompidou gasped at the sight of a prearranged and perfectly to scale model of the Eiffel Tower positioned on the relief map, looming up over what in real life would have been a gigantic, thousand-foot rill.

For all the hours astronauts logged inside the simulators, often the crews slated to fly the upcoming missions did not log the most. Each three-man Apollo crew had a three-man backup crew, and each three-man backup crew had what was known as a three-man support crew. The work of each of these crews differed considerably. The prime crewmen, of course, were the elite members of this trio of trios, chosen more than two years earlier to climb into the spacecraft and actually fly the flight for which all three teams were preparing. The problem, NASA knew, was that when the time for liftoff came, one of these treasured men might not be ready to make the trip. Even in a near-half-billion-dollar enterprise like a moon flight, it was never possible to

The film's simulator room.

control all variables, and a broken leg or a sudden flu or a hundred other mishaps could easily slip through NASA's perimeter. For this reason, a backup crew would be designated, which would go through the same drilling, the same rehearsals, the same grueling gauntlet as the prime crew, all with NASA's fervent hope that none of the three men on this team would ever have to use the knowledge he was amassing. The only consolation for a pilot tapped for so thankless a job was that, according to NASA's rotation rules, the backup crew for one flight would automatically be promoted to the prime crew three missions later.

If backup crew work was without any immediate payoff, a support-crew assignment could be even worse. With personal appearances to be booked for the prime crew, launch-day hotel rooms to be booked for their families, and a huge number of administrators, dignitaries, and other VIPs to be greeted and squired in the days leading up to a mission, somebody had to do all the social planning, and the support crew generally got the nod. So ignoble was this work that support crews were not even deemed worthy of a consolation lunar flight somewhere down the line. The most junior astronauts in the most recent classes were picked for these assignments, and their space futures probably lay *far* in the future, somewhere in the Skylab or shuttle programs still being planned.

The Apollo 13 actors on the steps outside a spacecraft simulator.

Between the prime and backup crews, the competition for training time in the simulators was fierce. NASA rules made it clear who got priority—and it was not the understudies. As a practical matter, however, the prime crew didn't always actually log the most hours. With all the public relations demands the Agency and the media made on their time, the first-string astronauts often had fewer opportunities than they would have liked to do the jobs they were hired to do. The more high-profile the pending mission, the more the glad-handing and ribbon-cutting, and the more opportunities the backup team had to train. On some flights, like Apollo 11, the first moon landing, the understudy astronauts even began playfully plotting against the prime team. One afternoon about a month before launch, Jim Lovell and Fred Haise, the backup commander and the LEM pilot, were wrapping up several hours in the LEM simulator when Neil Armstrong and Buzz Aldrin showed up for some training time of their own. As the two subordinates were preparing to relinquish the cockpit to the two stars, Haise caught his toe on a piece of loose flooring, lost his balance, and stumbled forward.

Before the prime crew could assume the controls of the simulator, Haise knew, the technicians would have to be alerted so that the uneven deck could be hammered back in place. No sooner did he make a mental note of that, however, than he made a devilish note of something else: if a member of the

The movie's simulator room.

The three prime crew members of the real Apollo 13 stand by to participate in water-egress training in a tank at the Kennedy Space Center in January 1970. *(NASA)*

backup crew lost his balance inside the simulator, who was to say a member of the prime crew wouldn't also? And if a member of the prime crew took such a tumble, who's to say he'd be fit to fly to the moon at all? The backup LEM pilot smiled at the thought, then shook it off, and hurried out of the ship to report the problem to the simulator technicians so that the floor could be repaired. When Neil Armstrong and Buzz Aldrin climbed inside, they didn't have to give their footing a second thought.

Where all of the astronauts in training did have to think about their footing was in another favored flight simulator: the zero-g trainer. For all of the otherworldly sensations a pilot would experience the moment he left Earth, none was more extraterrestrial than weightlessness. Even in the Mercury and Gemini spacecraft, which had barely enough room to stretch comfortably, much less to float around, the absence of gravity could be unsettling. Objects with earthly weight would suddenly drift in an ethereal float; an astronaut's arm resting absently in his lap would stubbornly rise to eye level before the pilot could catch it and tuck it away. During Apollo missions, on which there would be two spacious ships, a tunnel connecting both, and seemingly all the room in the world to float about, things would be even more disorienting.

To prepare for this cosmic buoyancy, astronauts would train in a retrofitted, internally padded aircraft, a modified Boeing 707, known formally as the KC-135 and known less formally as the Vomit Comet. The principle behind the Vomit Comet was simple: if you dive a plane steeply enough and accelerate it fast enough, you can neutralize the force with which gravity is pulling on the vehicle, rendering the pilot, the crew, and every clipboard, pen, and coffee cup inside it weightless. The absence of gravity would not last long: a pilot could dive his plane at such high speeds for only about twenty-three seconds before the ground would begin looming forbiddingly in his windshield, requiring him to pull out of the dive and commence a sudden climb. When he did, the friendly zero-g environment instantly transformed into an oppressive two-g environment, causing an astronaut who weighed, say, 170 pounds on the ground to go from weighing nothing at all in the KC-135 to weighing 340 pounds. This, of course, explained the need for padding in the ship. For the astronauts to get anything at all from these intermittent flashes of no weight and great weight, between twenty and forty of these vertiginous parabolas would have to be flown over the course of just a few hours. This accounted for the name Vomit Comet.

Jim Lovell, with back to the camera, and Fred Haise practice their moonwalking skills. *(NASA)*

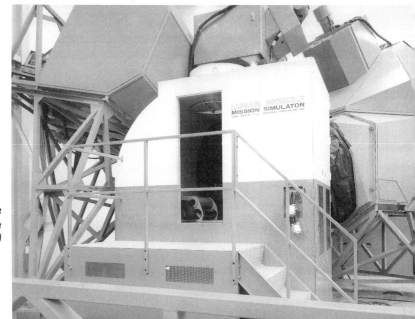

Exterior view of the Apollo lunar-module simulator. *(NASA)*

But what the KC-135 exacted from the pilots in terms of gastric distress, it paid them back tenfold in terms of piloting experience. Nowhere was this more evident than in the training regimen for the first extravehicular activities, or space walks, mission exercises that were confidently practiced during the Apollo program, but learned during the earlier Gemini program. Ed White, the pilot in the right-hand seat during the mission of Gemini 4, was the first American astronaut to venture outside his spacecraft. While the twenty minutes he spent in tethered float essentially went smoothly, he did encounter one stubborn—and potentially fatal—complication. Once he opened the hatch and maneuvered himself outside the ship, he had a monstrously difficult time wriggling back inside and getting the big, armored door shut again.

The problem, he discovered, was his space suit. White, five feet ten inches tall, had a hard enough time fitting comfortably inside the tiny Gemini cockpit. In a sealed pressure suit, inflated to capacity in the vacuum of space, he became even more ungainly. What's more, the more the suit inflated, the less dexterous an astronaut became, with his gait limited to a near waddle and his upper-body dexterity limited to gross motor movements at best. At the end of his space walk, when the time came to slam and seal the hatch above his head, the awkward, overinflated White found that he was repeatedly slamming it on the *top* of his head. Only with enormous effort and more than a few cranial thumps did he manage to pull it down and get it closed. When the astronaut returned to Earth, he promptly buttonholed Dave Scott, the six-foot-tall Gemini 8 pilot who was scheduled for the next American space walk.

"Dave," White said, "you're going to have to get this thing figured out, and you're going to have to get it figured out in zero g."

Scott, heeding the warning, promptly booked himself as much time in the KC-135 as NASA would allow and, working with a mock-up of the Gemini spacecraft, immediately discovered that if the hatch was rough for the shorter White, it was almost impossible for him. Ultimately, the spacecraft engineers had to rig up a lever and cable system that would allow Scott to position himself in his right-hand seat and then crank the hatch shut, pressing himself farther and farther into his couch as the door pressed harder and harder against his head. Nine months later, the makeshift device got him into space.

Valuable as zero-g flying was, of course, it had its limitations. Bobbing about inside a parabolic airplane might teach you a lot about maneuvering your body around your ship, but it taught you nothing at all about maneuvering the ship itself. In the case of the Apollo program, one of the best tools for mastering this skill was the inelegantly named and less elegantly designed Lunar Landing Training Vehicle, or LLTV. The LLTV was essentially a stand-in for a real lunar module, one that was able to do something no other simulator could: fly. Little more than a two-ton, open-air, four-legged chassis with a seat and a control stick, the LLTV was equipped with twin hydrogen-peroxide rocket engines that could lift the entire weight of the craft, a jet engine that could lift five-sixths of it, and sixteen miniature maneuvering thrusters. An astronaut training for a lunar landing would climb inside this improbable contraption, light the rocket engines, and climb to about a thousand feet. He would then light the jet engine, which, neutralizing all but 675 pounds of the ship's weight, would reduce the overall pull of gravity to roughly what it would be on the moon. Controlling the altitude of the ship with a throttle attached to the rocket engines, the astronaut would then try to plant the craft safely on the ground. To make the experience as real as possible, the ship was designed to sense even the gentlest breeze and then gimbal the jet engine to counteract it, simulating the windless conditions the astronaut would encounter on the moon.

With its low speed and equally low altitude, the LLTV seemed like a comparatively safe ship, but in fact, it was dangerous. First of all, despite its gimballing engine, the unaerodynamic craft was extremely susceptible to wind gusts, causing it to totter dangerously at heights one hundred stories above the ground. More important, to reduce overall weight, the vehicle was supplied with just two minutes of rocket fuel for the trip up and barely one minute of rocket and jet fuel for the trip down. Overstay your welcome in the sky and you could find yourself falling like an anvil to an earthly surface that did not have the moon's forgiving one-sixth gravity.

On occasion, even NASA's best astronauts had to learn these lessons the hard way.

Early in May of 1968, five months before Wally Schirra, Donn Eisele, and Walt Cunningham were scheduled to fly the first, modest, Earth-orbital mission aboard Apollo 7, the signs were already pointing to a moon landing as early as the following summer. While Schirra's crew enjoyed the media spotlight in anticipation of their autumn launch, Neil Armstrong, the presumed commander of the July 1969 flight, labored in something much closer to obscurity, spending this week at Ellington Air Force Base in Houston,

The artificial lunar module on the make-believe lunar surface constructed for the movie.

flying the Lunar Landing Training Vehicle. Armstrong was no novice at the LLTV, having taken the spindly ship up twenty times before. Among astronauts, only Pete Conrad, the planned commander of Apollo 12, approached Armstrong in LLTV experience, and he had just over half Armstrong's time.

Approaching the familiar, buglike ship this day, Armstrong looked a bit like an insect himself, with white coveralls, white helmet, a black, eye-exaggerating visor, and a black, mandiblelike communications mask. Hauling himself up into the pilot's gondola, he sat in the open-air seat like a construction worker in a backhoe and, without ceremony, lit his engines. Instantly, the LLTV began emitting the *chuffing* of a steam locomotive and slowly wrestled itself off the tarmac and into the air. Working the stick in front of him, Armstrong took the simulator up to about 500 feet and held it there. This was as good a place as any from which to begin a simulated lunar landing, and Armstrong allowed the vehicle to hover for another few seconds while he lit his jet engine to begin his downward trip.

For the first few seconds of Armstrong's descent, the LLTV behaved as it should. All at once, however, at an altitude of 210 feet, the craft began to pitch sickeningly forward, picking up speed alarmingly as it did so. Armstrong

Lunar-landing training vehicle. *(NASA)*

immediately engaged his attitude thrusters to neutralize the pitch, but though the thrusters fired, they seemed to have no effect. Even as Armstrong fought to stabilize the ship, it pitched hard to the right, flying essentially on its side. With the LLTV now toppled to starboard, the rocket engines on its underside that were supposed to keep it aloft fired uselessly to port. On the tarmac, observers turned and pointed; in Armstrong's headset, the roar of the engines drowned out any helpful advice that might be coming from the ground; in the open cockpit of the vehicle, the pilot could sense his already modest 210-foot altitude beginning to drop precipitously. With barely seconds to go before he fell to the ground, Armstrong reached for his ejection lever, gave it a hard pull, and launched himself away from the falling craft. An instant later, the LLTV crashed and exploded in a field adjacent to the airstrip.

Armstrong parachuted to safety a few hundred yards away.

Neil Armstrong would later climb into other LLTVs and pilot them through other, more successful simulated missions. Fourteen months later, he would climb into an authentic LEM for an authentic lunar landing and pull that off almost flawlessly as well. Before he did, however, Wally Schirra, who had done so much to determine the cause of the fire that killed the crew of the first planned Apollo mission, would investigate the reasons for the crash that almost killed the commander of the first lunar landing. Ultimately, Schirra would conclude, "The primary cause of the accident was that the vehicle entered a region of flight where aerodynamic moments overpowered the control system in use, such that attitude control was lost."

That was the long explanation. The short translation: a wind blew the ship off-balance. Neil Armstrong, Pete Conrad, and all of the men who would follow them moonward knew that they could live comfortably with that conclusion. Of all the perils they would face on their way to the lunar surface, wind would not be among them.

The Apollo command-module simulator is still located in the town of Cape Canaveral. To find it, however, you don't go to the local space center anymore. There was a time when you did, but not now. Now you go to the local industrial park—an undistinguished stretch of parking lots and alleyways broken up by boxy buildings serving mostly as light-industry plants, wholesale inventory outlets, and warehouses of varying sizes.

You don't know you're approaching a command-module simulator as you step inside one of these hangarlike buildings. Indeed, you don't know you're approaching much of anything at all. The warehouse is full of discarded equipment—much of it covered by tattered tarps—and if one of the big mounds of silent machinery has any richer a history than the others, it's not evident from a single look. Indeed, if someone wasn't here to guide you to the correct corner of the room and then point out the flaking legend on the flank of the machine—APOLLO SIMULATOR—you'd miss it altogether.

As you reach the tall stack of hardware, you're tempted to climb inside. But that's not so easy a matter, since the cockpit, supported by hollow metal cabinets that were once filled with computers and cables and knots of electronics, is a good ten feet off the ground. During its useful life, the humming, blinking, new-car-smelling module was accessible by a rolling metal stairway like the ones fighter pilots use to climb into their jets. Those days, however, are long gone, and a wooden ladder propped against the side of the simulator now does the job.

When you climb up the ladder, it's a simple matter to hold on to a bar above the hatch, swing your legs ahead of you, and hoist yourself inside the cockpit. A generation of grime covers the floor of the craft, just where you would lie if you pulled yourself into one of the recumbent, three-abreast seats. The instrument panels—the ones that are left—are covered so thickly with the same twenty years of dirt that the grains have sunk into the joints of the switches, giving them an arthritic resistance as they are flipped back and forth. Many of the switches—along with the panels that held them—are gone altogether, and a glance at various parts of the dashboard affords a view straight through the cockpit and into the dark forward portions of the ship.

Given the simulator's missing guts and its lowly state, there's not much to do once you've settled into your seat beyond toying with a few knobs and trying not to inhale too much of the dust you stirred up when you entered. You almost wonder why you bothered climbing inside.

Almost immediately, you realize why you bothered. These seats, after all, were not always so dirty; these switches were not always so gritty; this air was once clean and particulate free and quite nearly antiseptic. And when the air *was* clear, when the switches *were* clean, it wasn't you reclining in these seats.

It was Buzz Aldrin and it was Pete Conrad and it was Dave Scott and it was Jim Lovell and it was Neil Armstrong and it was Frank Borman and it was Gene Cernan and it was Tom Stafford and it was Stu Roosa and it was Fred Haise. And they weren't here to look and poke and play with a museum

Jim Lovell learns to handle the equipment he would have carried on the surface of the moon. Astronaut Fred Haise is standing in the left background. *(NASA)*

piece. They were here to do nothing less than learn how to fly to the moon. Over the course of several magnificent years from the late 1960s to the early 1970s, they did that very thing. And from the vantage point of your dusty couch, you realize that if it weren't for this sad, chipped hulk you climbed into today, they couldn't have made the trip. When you recognize that, you forget the dust.

Apollo 9
CONFIDENTIAL COCKPIT RECORDINGS

Jim McDivitt: commander
Dave Scott: command module pilot
Rusty Schweickart: lunar module pilot

MARCH 6, 1969

75 hours, 15 minutes, 15 seconds, mission elapsed time

McDivitt, Scott, and Schweickart are in Earth orbit for the first test flight of the lunar module. Their schedule is crowded.

McDIVITT: Oh, boy! Tomorrow we have two and a half hours to do everything we did today plus a P51 in the morning. It took us just two and a half hours today to do that—just to get ready.

SCHWEICKART: Yes, but we've—

McDIVITT: What we ought to do is get up an hour earlier and get a little more organized.

SCHWEICKART: Why in the hell do they put the whole job in one day? What's the rush?

SCOTT: Because we're liable to die.

SCHWEICKART: Oh, shoot! We're liable to die.

MARCH 8, 1969

126 hours, 04 minutes, 41 seconds, mission elapsed time

The lunar-module maneuvers are complete, and the crew is sealing up their command module and preparing to continue the mission in that ship alone.

SCOTT: One hundred twenty-six hours and four minutes. Now here's where the flight planner really did something right. He gave us twenty minutes to stow the magazines and cameras.

SCHWEICKART: Oh, you're kidding. *(Laughter)* And they gave us fifteen minutes to restow the tunnel alone.

McDIVITT: That's a hell of a—isn't it?

SCOTT: You know how long they gave us to unstow and install the SO sixty-five cameras? Fifty minutes. That's toward the end of the mission.

McDIVITT: Figured we'd be tired.

SCOTT: I'm going to—I'm going to go in a corner and write things down about the rendezvous because I don't have anybody [on the ground] to talk to yet about what I was doing.

McDIVITT: That's what I wanted to do. That's what I started to do last night and I never got it done.

SCOTT: I'm afraid I'm going to forget some of those things.

McDIVITT: Like that *vroom-vroom* of the descent engine.

152 hours, 44 minutes, 39 seconds, mission elapsed time

The mission is in its seventh day, and the crew, like most crews, has begun to grow weary of the freeze-dried rations in the spacecraft's larder.

HOUSTON: Apollo 9, Houston.

McDIVITT: Go ahead.

HOUSTON: Roger, what do you want me to put on your steak that I'm going to have for you tonight?

McDIVITT: Nothing, just eat it—just raw—well, not raw, just medium rare. But don't put anything on it. You'll ruin the taste.

HOUSTON: *(Laughing)* Okay.

McDIVITT: But taste it good for us, will you?

HOUSTON: Will do.

SCHWEICKART: Listen, you may be having steak, but I've got a larger choice of things right here. I have day six, meal C; I have day six, meal C; I have day six, meal C; I even have day six, meal D.

The astronauts click off the air and gather up their food packets for dinner.

McDIVITT: Hey, I've got a great idea. Why don't we all go up and sit and watch the—watch the world go by.

SCOTT: Okay.

SCHWEICKART: What are we having for dinner?

McDIVITT: Banana pudding. Oh! What happened to the chocolate pudding? Vanilla pudding? Shoot, I'd eat anything but banana pudding. *(Examining other food packet)* Oh, spaghetti! Banana pudding and spaghetti.

SCHWEICKART: I've never had the spaghetti. How is it?

McDIVITT: It's not bad. I'd recommend it for an upset stomach.

SCHWEICKART: Does it taste like what it says?

McDIVITT: Yes, I thought it—I thought it was really not too bad. It's rather palatable, as a matter of fact.

SCHWEICKART: Boy, didn't that steak sound good tonight?

SCOTT: What a dirty guy! Just . . . think of . . . big . . . big . . . steaks . . .

NASA's zero-gravity aircraft—an air-to-air photograph of the KC-135, a modified Boeing 707. *(NASA)*

4

The Vomit Comet

THE MAKING OF THE MOVIE

Tom Hanks was not surprised one day in 1994 when he found he weighed more than 350 pounds. Ordinarily, of course, Hanks weighs barely half that, but suddenly doubling that figure did not trouble him a bit. After all, in a few seconds, he knew he'd weigh nothing at all.

Hanks was not the only person who found the scale fluctuating so wildly that day. So did Kevin Bacon and Gary Sinise and Bill Paxton. And so did Imagine Films director Ron Howard and executive producer Todd Hallowell. The four actors and two filmmakers were spending their morning aboard a retrofitted Boeing 707—known familiarly as the NASA KC-135 weightlessness trainer, and even more familiarly as the Vomit Comet. Their ride today would be the first of many in preparation for filming some of the most dramatic—and certainly most demanding—scenes in the movie *Apollo 13*.

When Ron Howard and Imagine producer Brian Grazer first decided to make a feature film out of the story of the 1970 Apollo 13 lunar mission, they faced a number of challenges: how to transform six days of lunar history into two and a half hours of screen time without sacrificing either scientific accuracy or audience-pleasing drama; how to persuade a public accustomed to tales of America's long series of successes in space that its most heroic mission might have been the one historians have long called a failure; most important, how to bring the images of that gripping moon flight to film in a way that would do justice both to the moviemakers

Ron Howard and Tom Hanks in the Vomit Comet.

and to the story of Apollo 13. For a director attempting to tell the tale of any space mission, no technical challenge is greater than this last one, and nothing *makes* it more of a challenge than the business of re-creating weightlessness.

From the moment astronauts enter orbit around Earth, the phenomenon of zero g does the most to make the experience literally otherworldly. A booster flinging a spacecraft into orbit operates little differently from a gun firing a bullet in an open field. Propelled by the explosive force of its gunpowder charge, the bullet flies from the barrel at hundreds or sometimes thousands of miles per hour. In theory, even the slowest bullet could remain in flight forever, since, as no less an authority than Isaac Newton observed, an object in motion will tend to remain in motion unless acted on by an outside force. A bullet is an object in motion; the problem is, it is also acted upon by a pair of outside forces: gravity and atmospheric friction. No sooner does the little missile leave the gun than the drag of the air and the tug of Earth combine to begin slowing it down, causing it to plop harmlessly to the ground less than a mile from where it began its flight.

But suppose you had a gun so big that the bullet you fired could climb a hundred miles above ground and reach a speed of 17,500 miles per hour? With the atmosphere now far below, no air would retard the projectile's flight, and much of the energy that's usually robbed from it would be preserved. What's more, though gravity would continue to pull on the bullet, the enormous speed at which the little plug of metal was traveling would prevent it from being pulled back to Earth. No sooner would the tug of the planet cause the bullet to begin to fall back to the ground than the curvature of Earth would cause the ground to fall away from it. No matter how far the bullet flew and no matter how much its trajectory bent, the receding Earth would continue to bend with it, leaving it in a sort of permanent, circular plummet, falling around and around the planet without ever falling *into* it.

For any passenger riding aboard—or inside—the speeding projectle, this circumglobal plunge would produce a singularly curious effect. If a body falls fast enough and surrenders to the pull of the planet completely enough, the pull is essentially neutralized. Inside a missile in free fall, loose objects, cargo, and even the pilots lose all weight, floating effortlessly upward and hovering in place even as the projectile carrying them continues to dive.

For the most part, only when human beings began traveling in space was free-fall weightlessness experienced in any significant way. Long before that, however, pilots discovered that they could simulate the phenomenon for brief periods simply by flying their planes steeply upward, tipping them over at the top of the climb, and plunging toward Earth at hundreds of miles per hour. The sensation of weightlessness would last only twenty or thirty seconds before the pilot would have to pull back out of the dive, instantly converting his buoyant zero-g environment into a crushing two g's. But for those remarkable seconds before the climb, gravity could indeed be conquered.

In 1957, when NASA began choosing the astronauts who would make the nation's first tentative trips into space, flight planners concluded that the brief flashes of weightlessness attainable aboard an aircraft could go a long way toward preparing pilots for the more enduring zero g they would experience aboard a spacecraft. Shortly afterward, the Vomit Comet was born.

Thirty-seven years later, when Ron Howard and his creative team at Imagine Films decided to make the movie *Apollo 13*, they concluded that the same phenomenon could help them tell the tale of what three of those NASA pilots experienced on one of the space agency's most remarkable trips.

Ron Howard, Tom Hanks, Kevin Bacon, Gary Sinise, Bill Paxton, and Todd Hallowell sat six abreast in airline seats at the back of NASA's KC-135 weightlessness trainer.

The six men looked for all the world like astronauts—and indeed, to the uninformed observer, they might even have *been* astronauts. Like astronauts, they were dressed in army green, zipper-front, NASA-issue jumpsuits. Like astronauts, they were wearing lace-up, heavy-gauge pilot's boots. And, like astronauts, they were off on a mission the likes of which none of them had ever experienced before. Unlike astronauts, however, they were very nervous about it—and what they had seen and experienced already today told them that they had plenty of reason to be.

The interior of the plane in which they were riding, for example, had been completely gutted—leaving a hollow tube from the rear end of the fuselage to the front—and the bulkheads on all sides had been covered with a thick, neoprene padding. When a floor is thickly padded, of course, it's a sign that someone's in danger of taking a fall; when walls are thickly padded, it's a sign that someone could be lurching sideways; when the ceilings are thickly padded . . . it didn't pay to think about what *that* would be protecting you from. Earlier in the morning, NASA medics had prescribed all of the men a potent combination of scopolamine and Dexedrine, a powerful medicinal cocktail that leaves even the most drug-resistant subjects feeling slightly disoriented,

The KC-135 preparing for a sunrise flight.

slightly edgy, and curiously uninhibited. What it also leaves them feeling, however, is unusually resistant to motion sickness—a good thing to feel in a plane that will be flying so acrobatically that someone has felt it necessary to pad the ceilings. In the breast pockets of all six men's suits were twin pieces of flight equipment that the NASA technicians called the "airman's corsage"—two plastic bags with sealable tops that could be pulled hurriedly out in case the scopolamine and Dexedrine failed to do their jobs.

At the moment, the KC-135 with the Imagine Films crew aboard was heading southeast from Ellington Air Force Base in Houston, out toward a distant spot in the Gulf of Mexico. This destination, too, was a cause of more than a little unease. There is almost no plane NASA is afraid to fly, almost no missile it's afraid to launch. When Agency planners decide that the refitted jet it's transporting you in today can fly its assigned mission only out over remote, boatless waters hundreds of miles from populated areas, you know they're not flying it casually.

At the same time the KC-135 was flying *out,* it was also flying up—up to about 36,000 feet, or about 6.8 miles. Anyone who has ever flown in a commercial jet airliner, has, of course, climbed to about 36,000 feet; few people, however, have ever flown in a commercial airliner intended to tip over into a steep dive the moment it reaches the top of its climb. Diving planes, of course, can become stressed planes, and stressed planes can become damaged planes. When a plane becomes damaged at 36,000 feet, one of the things it can do is depressurize. Nearly seven miles above sea level, depressurization is not a good thing, and several days before, Howard, Hanks, Bacon, Sinise, Paxton, and Hallowell had sampled what a sudden loss of pressure miles above ground would feel like to an unprotected flier.

This unpleasant test had been conducted at the medical center at Ellington in a sealed, hypobaric chamber that looked like a large, walk-in refrigerator with windows. Along the walls of the chamber were straight, hard, backless benches facing one another across the room. Before being okayed for the KC-135 mission, the Imagine team had been brought into this room, seated on the benches, and issued clipboards, pens, and—disquietingly—oxygen masks. On cue, they were told, they would don the masks, the door would be sealed, and the pressure inside the chamber would steadily be lowered. When the atmospheric gauges outside the room indicated that the pressure and oxygen content of the air inside had dropped to about what it would be at 36,000 feet, the six subjects would be instructed to remove their masks and, breathing only the relative scattering of O_2 molecules available to them, try to answer a few simple arithmetic problems printed on a questionnaire, before the telltale symptoms of oxygen deprivation—nausea, claustrophobia, dizziness, loss of peripheral vision—overcame them.

The test was a familiar one to military pilots, but utterly unfamiliar to moviemakers. Nevertheless, at a sign from an Ellington medic—stationed prudently on the other side of the window—the door was slammed shut, the atmosphere pumped out, and the men instructed to doff their masks. One by one they complied, warily inhaled the rarefied air, and with their faculties so far undiminished, quickly fell to work answering the questions on the sheet.

All six eventually grew at least a little queasy from the loss of oxygen, but all six finished the assigned task successfully, emerging from the chamber happily, if woozily.

As their reward for undergoing that dubious exercise, they found themselves undergoing today's dubious exercise—sitting in the back of a gutted, padded jet, heading out to Gulf waters far south of Texas for a few high-speed power dives.

Shortly before arrival at the designated test site, a NASA flight supervisor made his way to the rear of the plane and addressed Howard and his crew, calling out over the roar of the engines. Much of what he said had been explained to the group before, but with weightlessness now only minutes away, it bore repeating.

"We're going to be there anytime now," the supervisor half-shouted, "and I want you all to remember a few things. It is not recommended that you leave your seats and try to float on the first series of parabolas. Just stay where you are and allow the plane to go through two or three cycles, so you can get the feel of both zero g and two g." Howard, Hanks, Hallowell, and the rest looked at one another and nodded. "If you feel sick," the flight officer went on, "try to get yourself stabilized in one position before using your airsickness bag. Remember, anything that's released in the cabin will continue to float about until gravity gets ahold of it at the end of the parabola." The Imagine crew nodded at one another at that, too. "Finally, do not get so caught up in floating around that you forget to listen for the warning calls. When you hear someone shout the words 'Thirty down!' that means we're about to pull out of the dive and you should find something to hold on to. Otherwise, you'll hit the deck about three seconds later, and at twice your usual body weight, you'll hit it hard. Got it?"

The six men got it, nodded their heads to indicate so, and the flight director made his way back to his seat. For another minute or two, the KC-135 continued to drone ahead, banking a little one way, then a little the other, but otherwise doing nothing especially noteworthy. All at once, however, the engine pitch changed dramatically, and the big, empty 707 suddenly and sickeningly tipped down.

For the briefest instant, the passengers noticed nothing different inside their plane from what would happen inside any other plane that went into a sudden plummet. The loose ends of their seat belts dangled forward with the dive; the loose ends of their shoelaces did the same; their bodies hung heavily in their straps. Instantly, however, all that changed. As the passengers watched, amazed, the belts and laces snaked eerily back upward, floating in place as if they were floating in water; the sensation of weight vanished, causing the seat restraints, which a fraction of a second before had been digging uncomfortably into chests and waists, to hang loosely.

"Zero g!" one of the flight officers called out, and the passengers looked at one another and smiled. The interior of the KC-135 now resembled the interior of any spacecraft traveling in orbit. Bits of lint lost in the folds of the neoprene on the floor floated eerily upward; stacks of paper held in clipboards fanned outward; NASA test directors not belted into place like the Imagine crew levitated into the air.

The high-speed dive lasted for five seconds, ten seconds, fifteen, twenty, twenty-two, then finally the announcement went out. "Thirty down!" Almost as if in obedience to the call, the KC-135 reared back, its engines changed their pitch again, and the plane pointed its nose back up at the sky from which it had just come. The Imagine passengers, who only moments ago had felt buoyant as bubbles, were suddenly slammed back in their seats at twice their normal body weights, flattened into—and practically through—the springs

Tom Hanks, Ron Howard, Bill Paxton, Kevin Bacon, Gary Sinise, and Todd Hallowell in the Vomit Comet.

and cushions behind them. Their heads were pushed heavily into their head-rests; their arms were practically pinioned to their sides; their eyes seemed to weigh heavily in their skulls.

"Two g's," the officer said. This time the passengers did not look at one another and nod, not so much because they didn't want to, but because they barely could.

The KC-135 made two more such cycles over the next two minutes, alternately flattening its passengers with a gravity anvil and releasing them. Knowing what the dives and climbs would feel like made it easier for the six men to prepare for them, and being able to prepare for them made it seem more possible to maneuver around in them. When the third cycle was completed, no one in the back of the plane had yet ventured up from the safety of the seats, but now, as the fourth one was beginning, Bill Paxton unceremoniously reached up, released his belts with a metallic snap, and then, simply . . . began to float. Pushing cautiously away from his chair, he drifted slightly forward and looked over his shoulder to the other five with an encouraging smile. Howard, Hanks, Hallowell, Bacon, and Sinise looked back and, after an instant, released their own restraints.

For the next twenty seconds, the six men experienced a feeling unlike anything they'd ever felt before. Up vanished; down vanished; lateral direction lost its meaning. The ceiling of the KC-135 might just as easily have been the floor; the floor might as well have been the ceiling. They floated this way, breaststroked that way, somersaulted forward and backward. Then, after what seemed like an eyeblink, came the "Thirty down" call. Immediately, all six men planted their feet as best they could and braced themselves for the sudden reappearance of gravity. When it arrived, it was even worse than they had imagined, hitting with almost knee-buckling force after the twenty-three seconds of ethereal float. For about fifteen seconds, the passengers sweated out the plane's climb, then the familiar change in engine pitch returned, the familiar shift in orientation occurred, and the pull of gravity once again vanished.

Forty times that day the plane flew up and down, up and down, with the passengers' weight rising and falling accordingly, and forty times the passengers practiced their zero-g skills. As the final dive was under way, Howard floated up to the lead test officer, who had made these flights countless times before and who knew that by parabola forty, most first-timers were more than ready to call it a day and head back to base.

The crew in their command module cockpit in the KC-135. This photo was taken by Apollo 15 commander Dave Scott.

"I don't know how flexible the flight plan is," Howard called out over the engine roar, "but we're getting pretty good at this and the guys wanted to know if we could maybe try ten more."

The test officer, mildly surprised, radioed the request back to the cockpit, and the word came back that the movie crew was indeed okayed to go for ten more dives. Later, however, Gary Sinise would admit to friends on the ground that the original forty parabolas were probably enough for him. Of course, to the men in the plane, that was evident even before Sinise fessed up to it—as early as the forty-seventh or forty-eighth dive, in fact, when the actor who would play astronaut Ken Mattingly blanched a bit, swam off by himself, and after holding off as long as he could, reached hurriedly into the pocket of his jumpsuit. For the first and only time that day, the onboard medic noted for the record, somebody had gotten a chance to try out his airman's corsage.

The command module being loaded into the KC-135.

It would be several months before the team from Imagine Films would return to Ellington Air Force Base and the KC-135 weightlessness trainer. When they did, it would not be with a crew of just six, but with a crew of eleven—and this time, those eleven people would be bringing more than just their wonder. Along for the ride during this visit would be cameras and lights, pressure suits and helmets, monitors and shot lists, and two remarkably accurate replicas of the cockpits of the Apollo command module and lunar module. With the cockpits bolted in place inside the KC-135 cabin, the actors secured inside the cockpits, and Howard, his cameramen, and the rest of his film crew arrayed around them, a grueling month of filming inside NASA's notorious Vomit Comet began.

Over those four-plus weeks of flying—all of which were paid for by the moviemakers—the filming conditions would never be anything approaching ideal. The drone of the engines would be so loud that all of the dialogue would have to be rerecorded in a studio weeks later; the plane would be pushed so hard that at one point it would have to be grounded to repair potential cracks in its engine housing; the cast and crew would fly so often and endure so many thirty-down climbs that the off-hours they were allowed on the ground would be spent mostly tottering back to their hotel rooms and falling quickly asleep.

By any measure, however, the time they devoted to weightlessness flying appeared to have paid off. A few days after the film team went down to Houston, the first raw footage from their flights was shipped back to Universal Studios in Los Angeles. On the *Apollo 13* set, the cast and crew that had stayed behind gathered around a monitor to watch. Among the people present that day was astronaut and technical consultant Dave Scott, commander of the 1971 Apollo 15 lunar-landing mission.

As the scenes from the KC-135 cabin played out on the monitor—with Tom Hanks somersaulting through the tunnel that connected the command module and the lunar module, Bill Paxton spinning his sunglasses weightlessly toward the camera, Kevin Bacon releasing a squirt of orange juice into the zero-g cabin and playfully catching the mercurylike globules in his mouth— the crowd watched silently.

When the clip at last ended, Scott said wonderingly, "I was up there three times, and I can tell you, what I saw on that monitor is what I experienced in space."

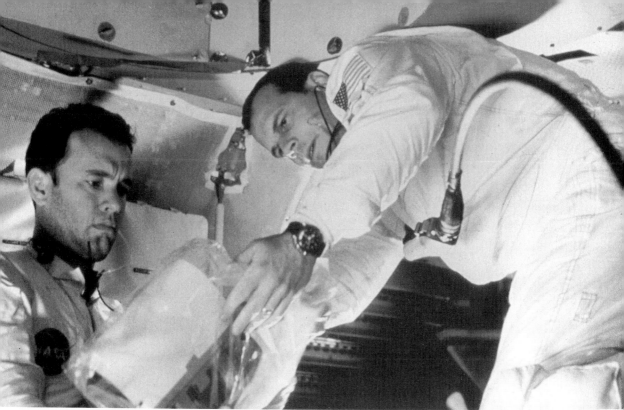

Tom Hanks and Bill Paxton in zero gravity, with makeshift lithium-hydroxide filter.

Tom Hanks and Bill Paxton after the accident during the lunar-module emergency power-up.

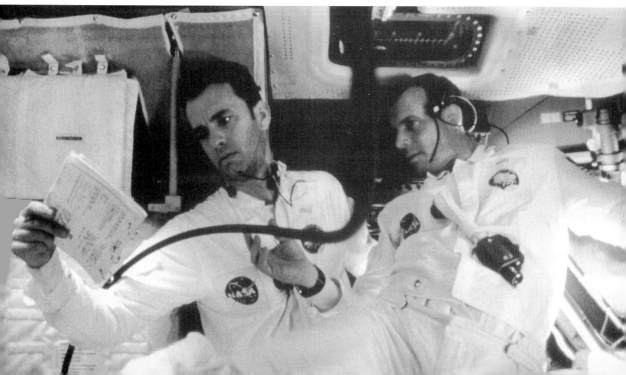

Kevin Bacon and Tom Hanks during liftoff of Apollo 13.

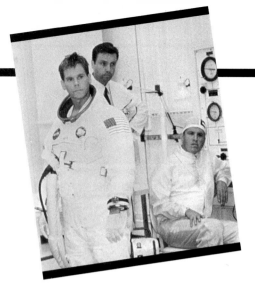

5

On Your Way to the Moon

What is it like to command a Saturn 5 as it leaves the ground and heads off toward the moon?

It's when they step on your shoulder that you know they mean business. They did a lot of things to you during training, but until today, no one had ever stepped on your shoulder before. Certainly, you don't object to somebody stepping on your shoulder this morning. Truth be told, you're kind of grateful for it. In a few hours, the giant bells of the Saturn 5's giant F-1 engines 363 feet below your back are going to begin vomiting hellfire with a thrust exceeding 7.5 million pounds, and when they do, anything that's not nailed down, strapped down, or bolted into place is going to be shaken to rubble. Virtually every other piece of cargo going aloft this morning was safely stowed days or even weeks earlier. You, however, only stepped out of the rattly metal elevator thirty-six stories above the sands of Cape Canaveral a few minutes ago and have only now settled into your canvas and aluminum couch. If the launch-pad supervisors and gantry technicians—"pad rats" you long ago learned to call them—believe it's necessary to press a sterile, bootie-clad foot against your shoulder while pulling with both hands to cinch your restraints tight enough for launch, you're not about to complain.

When the pad rats finish their work, you'll have a bit of idle time to contemplate what's ahead of you today, but considering that the main event of the morning is still hours away, you've gotten quite a bit accomplished already. On a launch day like today, when liftoff is scheduled for slightly before noon, Deke knocks on your door in the Cape Canaveral crew quarters at the near-indecent hour of 4 A.M. to wake you up and roust you out of bed. All things considered, you find you slept surprisingly well, but the moment you hear the *tap-tap-tap* outside your small, dormlike room, you open your eyes, sit up, and plant your feet on the floor. This is not, you realize, a morning on which anybody will grant you a request for just fifteen more minutes of sack time.

You don't say much to the other two men who will be riding with you today when you bump into them in the hall. First of all, you're still not fully awake. Second, what *would* you say? On this morning of all mornings, you don't want to sound sentimental, you don't want to sound banal, you don't want to sound even vaguely nervous. But nothing you can come up with at the moment doesn't carry at least a hint of all three. You're going to be spending the better part of the next two weeks with these two men, and if anything with the appropriate balance of profundity and swagger occurs to you, there'll be plenty of time to say it then.

You spend a few more minutes in the shower this morning than you normally would, partly because you realize it's your last one for two weeks and you want to enjoy it; partly because of an irrational, only half-conscious belief that if you get *especially* clean this morning, you can somehow minimize just how down-to-the-dermis dirty you're going to get before this whole enterprise is over. Stepping out and toweling off, you dress in the casual slacks and short-sleeve sport shirt you and the rest of the pilots have long since accepted as the uniform of the workplace, then head for the crew-quarters dining room.

Over the last seven days—ever since they put you in medical quarantine for the final week leading up to launch—you've been taking your meals in this most private of salons, and you've rather come to enjoy it. The chef they hired to manage the astronaut kitchen learned his trade in the galley of a tugboat, and the menus he comes up with—heavy on the meats, potatoes, pastas, and

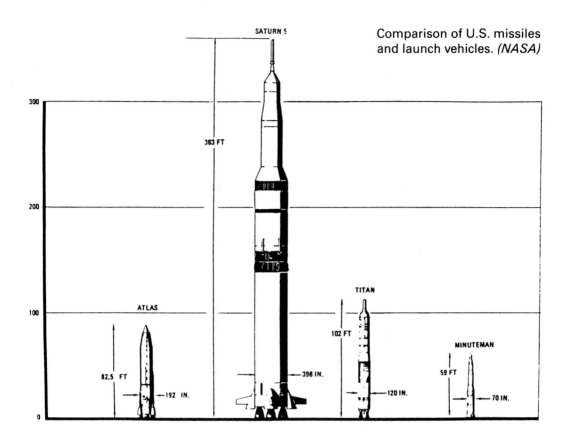

SATURN 5

Comparison of U.S. missiles
and launch vehicles. *(NASA)*

363 FT

TITAN

ATLAS

102 FT

MINUTEMAN

82.5 FT

396 IN.

59 FT

192 IN.

120 IN.

70 IN.

chickens, light on the salads and greens and fruits—suit your appetite exactly.
Today, you know before you arrive, the chef will be turning out the traditional
morning-of-launch fare—steak, eggs, toast, juice, and coffee—and on most
mornings you'd be looking forward to it. But as you approach the dining room
this morning, you notice for the first time that you're not quite as hungry as
you'd imagined you'd be. You wonder if your crewmates feel the same.

Of course, you and your two fellow pilots aren't the only ones whose
breakfast needs will have to be taken care of this morning. Deke is here, just
as he's always been here throughout most of the Mercury flights, from 1961 to
1963, all of the Gemini flights, from 1965 to 1966, and every one of the Apollo
flights, since 1968. Strictly speaking, you could probably get off the ground
without Deke around for breakfast, but you'd sooner fly without your helmet
than without the man the Agency knows as the director of flight crew
operations and you and your fellow pilots know simply as chief astronaut.

Also here today are three other men who slept in the same quarters you and your crewmates did last night, got up at the same time you did this morning, and dressed in the same country-club clothes you're wearing now. From a distance, these three men could almost *be* you and your crewmates—and in a sense they are. For the last two years, they've trained just as hard as you have for this mission, practiced the flight plan just as tirelessly, and if anything had happened to you in the last few days or weeks—a broken leg, a sudden flu, a fall off a ladder while hanging a picture at home—one of them would be going in your place today. NASA likes to think of all six of you as essentially interchangeable, but this morning the difference between the two groups is clear—if only in the gusto with which the three of them seem to be attacking their breakfast. You don't envy your backup crew the earthbound workday they'll be plodding through today while you rocket off to the moon; you do envy them their appetites.

Your next stop after your barely acknowledged meal is the suit-up room a few hundred feet down the hall. If there's anything you don't look forward to today, it's this. In the past—in your days as a Navy or Marine or Air Force pilot—preflight suit-up time was essentially private time, an opportunity to snap and tuck yourself into your coveralls, stop by the ready room for a quiet cup of coffee, then walk alone out to the tarmac, contemplating the work you would have to do in the jet that would be waiting for you there. Dressing for *this* flight is a whole different matter. There will be dozens of technicians hovering around you as you dress for your day, and with the exception of your Skivvies—which you're already wearing—there's not a single article of clothing you'll be permitted to don without their assistance. The press likes to compare the whole tedious suiting-up exercise to a sort of gladiator's ritual, but just what's so heroically Roman about standing passively in the middle of a room while a wardrobe team helps you through so humble a business as putting on your clothes has never been clear to you.

It's not just the helplessness of being dressed by committee, however, that makes the suiting-up unsettling. Rather, it's the realization that, as the last hose is snapped into place, as both gloves are twisted in their wrist rings, as your fishbowl-like helmet is ceremonially lowered over your head, the real act of leave-taking will officially have begun. You are still in the same building where you spent your night, you are still in the same room that you entered in your slacks and shirt, but you are no longer *of* that building or that room. The oxygen that now fills both your suit and your lungs comes not from the

Bill Paxton suiting up before liftoff.

Kevin Bacon suiting up.

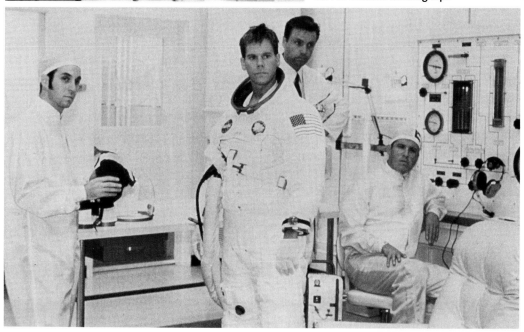

ambient atmosphere, but from a pressurized tank of pure O_2. The humidity in the suit is artificially maintained as well, as are the temperature and the pressure. For the next fourteen days, you will live your life in a series of such manufactured environments, transferring from the tiny cocoon of your space suit to the larger cocoon of your spacecraft to the fragile enclosure of your lunar module and then back to the suit for your moonwalk. Only at the end of the trip, when the spacecraft thumps into the South Pacific and the parachutes flatten on the water and you reach for the cabinet vent, twist it once, and feel the warm, wet ocean air rush into your ship, will you once again breathe the same atmosphere that the rest of humanity breathes. At the moment, that atmosphere still surrounds you, but you are already being denied so much as a molecule of it.

With the morning's wardrobe work at last done, the part of the launch-day ritual that feels vaguely gladiatorial even to you begins: the trip to the pad. As you leave the suit room and make your way down the hall, technicians and administrators line the walls, smiling and waving and reaching out to touch your hand as you pass. Every now and then, someone calls out a "Good luck" or a "Safe trip," but with your helmet in place and your portable atmosphere wooshing through it, you hear little but muffled babble. You make it a point to nod and wave in appreciation and even try flashing the occasional thumbs-up, but the thick, black gloves you'll be using four days from now to sift the soil of the lunar surface make even so simple a gesture more difficult than you'd expected.

Reaching the end of the hallway, you see someone push open a metal double door, and the early iridescent blue of a Florida dawn rushes in. Despite the inhuman hour, a crowd is out here, too, this one mostly media. Once again you wave and smile, but this group is less intent on wishing you well than on snapping your picture. The photo session will be frenzied, but also short: only about ten steps away from the door you just exited is the van you will enter for your trip to the launch pad.

As you approach the demitruck that has been waiting for you out here for most of the night, you notice that the back door is already open, and on its inside is the insignia of your mission—a three-foot-diameter replica of the same embroidered patch sewn to the chest of your pressure suit. Some months ago, you and your crewmates designed that patch, picking its central image—maybe an eagle, maybe a spacecraft, maybe a horse or a sailing ship—its principal colors, and even the position of your names and the size of

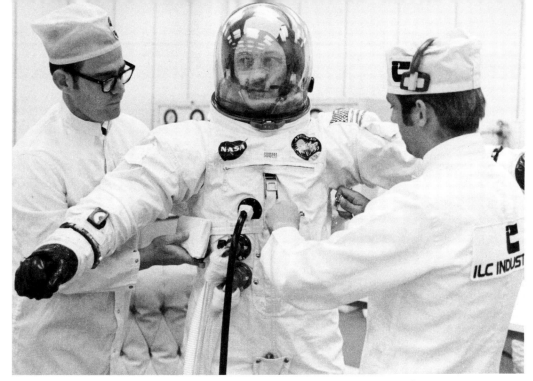

Technicians conducting space-suit checks to prepare astronaut John Swigert, the real Apollo 13 command module pilot, in April 1970. Swigert replaced Thomas Mattingly as a member of the crew after Mattingly was exposed to the measles. *(NASA)*

the lettering. If nothing else has made this morning's activities seem real to you, spotting this big painted re-creation of the little woven badge does. Over the years, you've seen these van plaques many times before, but always with other mission logos and other men's names. Today, the mission is yours, the logo is yours, and most significantly, one of the names is yours, too.

The ride in the van that today bears your imprimatur is brief, and with your climate-controlled body now sealed inside a climate-controlled vehicle, it is quiet, almost tranquil, as well. Only when you get to the gantry, ride up the elevator, walk down the gangplank to the spacecraft, and climb into your couch does the sense of serenity begin to dissolve. A few seconds later, when they start stepping on your shoulder, it vanishes altogether.

The wait in the spacecraft from the time they strap you in and seal the vaultlike hatch until the time you actually fly will be at least three hours—and it will only be that brief if the hundreds of men ministering to the 363-foot booster that now stands beneath you find no hardware glitch that has to be unraveled before the engines can safely be lit. Chances are they will—as you think back, you can't recall a flight on which they haven't—and this, you must admit, puzzles you a bit. The rocket you'll be riding today is known as a

At the Kennedy Space Center press site all eyes and cameras are focused on the Saturn 5 rocket carrying Apollo 8 astronauts Frank Borman, Jim Lovell, and William Anders on the first lunar orbital voyage. *(NASA)*

Cameras recording the movie launch of Apollo 13.

Saturn 5, and though the press generally refers to it as the most sophisticated flying machine ever built, you and your crewmates generally think of it as something much simpler and much more reliable: a gigantic flying fuel tank.

Poised on its pad and ready for launch, a Saturn 5 weighs a staggering 6.2 million pounds. Of that all-but-immeasurable weight, however, only an eggshell-like 430,000 pounds is the rocket itself. The rest—nearly 5.8 million pounds—is fuel: liquid oxygen, liquid hydrogen, and refined kerosene transfused into the gullet of the missile only hours before liftoff. By far, the lion's share of the rocket's weight is accounted for by its first stage, the so-called S-IC stage. Standing 138 feet tall, the S-IC houses five of the largest rocket engines ever built, which together produce an astounding 7.5 million pounds of thrust. Just one of these chemical motors generates more power than virtually any other rocket ever launched; together they quintuple the record.

Atop the first stage is the second stage, or the S-II. Measuring 81.5 feet from end to end, the S-II is a 95,000-pound, five-engine machine that, when fueled with liquid oxygen and liquid hydrogen, increases more than ten times in weight and generates 1.1 million pounds of thrust. Atop the S-II stage is the S-IVB, or third stage, a fifty-nine-foot-long, one-engine rocket with an unfueled weight of just 25,000 pounds and a thrust of 203,000. Atop all three of these stages is the ten-foot–seven-inch Apollo command module, which this morning is home to you and your crew. Two weeks from now, this tiny cone will be the only part of the mammoth Saturn 5 that will return, intact, to Earth.

This morning, the technicians find few glitches in this Brobdingnagian missile, and the wait atop it is a relatively short one. The ground keeps you updated as the time to launch ticks away, and you are surprised at how quickly you progress from T minus three hours to T minus two hours, to T minus sixty minutes, then thirty minutes, then just a quarter of an hour. After that, the remaining time melts even more fleetingly, until at T minus fifteen seconds, you're informed through your headset that the engine valves have opened in the mammoth first stage, and that the tons of fuel stored there have begun to flow. After another moment, you hear someone call out, "Ignition."

The detonation of kerosene and oxygen in the combustion chamber of a Saturn 5 booster should be a momentous event, but here, 363 feet above the controlled explosion, you sense nothing at all—or at first you don't. All at once, however, you notice that a single vibrating bass note has begun to shake

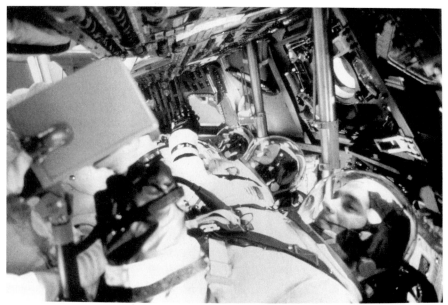

The crew during liftoff.

everything around you. The hardware harmonic is playing at way too low a register for you to hear it, but through the walls, through your couch, through your suit and your skin and your very viscera, you feel it. You've rehearsed many Saturn 5 launches before, and you know when to expect your engines to ignite, but you don't know what to expect when they do. This, you figure, has to be it.

But just because your engines have lit does not mean that your rocket is going anywhere. At the base of the booster, attached to the launch pad, are massive hold-down arms, multiton clamps designed to lock the rocket in place for several long seconds while the first-stage engines build up thrust. For a seemingly interminable time, the engines burn and the vehicle shakes and your couch shudders and the ship stands otherwise still. Then, finally, on the left side of the instrument panel, the engine thrust light goes on; to the right of it, the hold-down arms light goes off; and at long last, you feel yourself begin to rise.

The first thing a Saturn 5 rocket does as it climbs from the pad is something that by all rights it really oughtn't do: it leans. No matter how many times you've watched a Saturn fly, you've never quite gotten used to this. When 363 feet of incendiary device begins to struggle into the air just a

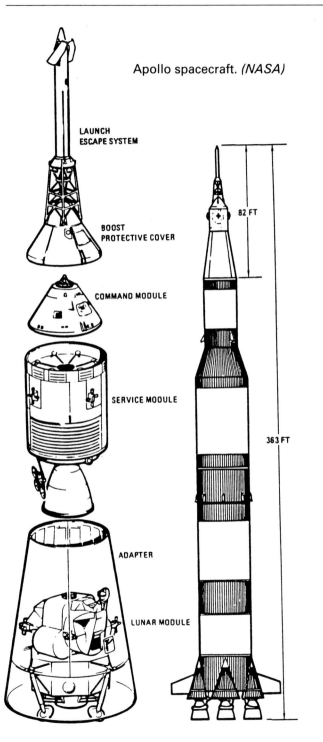

Apollo spacecraft. *(NASA)*

LAUNCH
ESCAPE SYSTEM

BOOST
PROTECTIVE COVER

COMMAND MODULE

SERVICE MODULE

ADAPTER

LUNAR MODULE

82 FT

363 FT

The Apollo 11 Saturn 5 space vehicle in May 1969 beginning its trip to launch complex 39A in preparation for the launch. *(NASA)*

few miles from one of the most densely populated urban centers in the Southeast, you'd really like to see it stand up straight. For the Saturn, however, at least a slight lean is necessary, if only so the rising booster can avoid grazing its skeleton-like gantry and damaging itself before it climbs as much as one hundred feet into the air. The tilt, you know, is a small one—little more than a degree to port. Nevertheless, it brought you up short the first time you saw it, and you made it a point long before today's launch to warn your wife about it and assure her that this is the way things are supposed to work.

Now, sitting atop the tower, you find that the tilt that seems so pronounced on the ground is barely discernible from inside the cockpit, and after just a few seconds, Houston calls up the welcome news that your spacecraft has cleared the tower and is on its way. Once this milestone is crossed, things begin to pick up dramatically. Though 7.5 million pounds of chemical oomph are bursting from your engine bells, the five tails of flame are still trying to lift 6.2 million pounds of missile—a not inconsiderable load. With each second the engines burn, however, hundreds and thousands of gallons of fuel are gulped, and as they are, the rocket gets lighter and lighter. The less the booster weighs, the faster a fixed thrust can move it, and as you lie back in your seat, you realize that *this* booster is now decidedly on the move.

As the Saturn 5 accelerates and climbs, it also begins to pitch forward, allowing it to rise through the atmosphere in a gentle incline that takes it eastward over the Atlantic as it moves upward into space. The more the missile tilts, of course, the more the cockpit does, too, and you notice with more than a little gratitude that your orientation has begun to change from the flat-backed pose of passive cargo to the upright posture of a pilot. For two and a half minutes, you pitch more and more comfortably forward, while the roar in your ears grows steadily louder and the vibration around you grows greater and greater. The entire ride atop the first-stage engines is intended to last only two and a half minutes, and when it ends, you ought to be no less than thirty-eight miles above the ground and moving no slower than six thousand miles per hour. Glancing at your mission clock, your altimeter, and your velocity indicator, you see that you are indeed adhering to that profile, and as the 150-second mark in your two-week lunar mission begins, you unconsciously hold on to the edge of your couch and brace yourself for the high-tech violence known as staging.

John Young, one of the astronauts who preceded you up here aboard Apollo 10, described staging as nothing short of a train wreck. And there is no reason it shouldn't be. With your ship and your body tearing along at just under two miles per second, the fuel that filled the first stage only minutes ago at last runs dry, and the chemical dynamos producing the power that propelled the ship suddenly shut off. When they do, the entire stack of hardware instantly slows, but your body, proceeding ahead with Newtonian stubbornness, doesn't. Accordingly, you find yourself suddenly and violently thrown forward in your straps—the same straps that were so carefully tightened by the technicians on the pad just a few hours earlier. Far behind you, explosive bolts fire, guillotining the first stage of the rocket from the second stage and allowing it to tumble like a 138-foot baton into the ocean.

For four interminable seconds, nothing happens while the remaining stages of your ship, with you aboard, continue to hurtle silently forward. If you kept on this way, you wouldn't hurtle for long, since with each passing millisecond, you lose a fraction of the thrust the discarded first stage worked so hard to provide. All at once, however, 140 feet to the rear, the five smaller engines of the second stage light, kicking you from behind with their 1.1

Tracy Reiner as Mary Haise and Kathleen Quinlan as Marilyn Lovell after liftoff.

million pounds of thrust. As suddenly as you were thrown forward in your seat a few moments ago, you are now slammed back in it, as the Saturn tries to move ahead and you, an object at relative rest, attempt to remain at rest. The Saturn wins this war, and you proceed along with your ship toward greater altitudes and higher speeds.

Though the Saturn's second stage has barely a seventh the thrust of the first, it has far more staying power than its bigger sibling, carrying enough fuel and consuming it stingily enough to burn for nearly six minutes. With the engines firing so long and the overall vehicle now so light, your speed and altitude increase almost exponentially—and so, you now notice, do the g forces. If you've flown up this way before, perhaps aboard one of the old Gemini Titans, you know all about g forces. The Titans were originally designed to carry not astronauts but warheads, and thus they did not have to take the comfort of any living payload into consideration. Accordingly, the speed with which the missiles flew and the trajectory they followed created a gravity load of almost eight g's. Going from a terrestrial weight of 170 or so pounds to an airborne weight of 1360 was something of a jolt, but the time you spent in the centrifuge during the months of training that led up to the launch made the experience tolerable, if not enjoyable.

Aboard the Saturn 5, things are different. Originally designed with only pilots in mind, the giant moonship climbs in a far more gentle arc and accelerates far more slowly than the Titan did. A gradual climb and a slow acceleration reduce the gravity crush significantly, lowering the load from eight g's to just four. Four g's, however, is still quite something, and as the pressure across your body grows, and your gross weight climbs above 600 pounds, you find yourself struggling just to draw a comfortable breath. Happily for you and your respiratory system, the second-stage g load does not last forever, and 359 seconds later, when you've climbed to 118 miles and your speed has reached a near-orbital 14,500 miles per hour, this stage, too, shuts down and falls away.

With the loss of the S-II, what's left of your magnificent Saturn 5 booster is not much: just a fifty-nine-foot, single-engine, third-stage rocket with the spacecraft affixed to its nose carrying you and your crew. At this point, you are well above the upper reaches of the atmosphere and are thus high enough to be—at least technically—in space. The problem is, you are not traveling fast enough to stay there. If you did nothing now, you would arc a few thousand miles eastward and then simply drop through the atmosphere somewhere on the other side of the planet, achieving nothing from today's thunderous launch but a transatlantic lob shot. For that reason, the instant the second stage falls away, the third stage kicks in, generating a final burst of thrust for two minutes, increasing your speed to 17,500 miles per hour, and placing you, at last, in orbit around Earth.

One of the least formal but most telling ways of judging the conscientiousness of the men who built your spacecraft is to wait until you get into orbit and look for what floats. The interior of a spacecraft, at least in theory, should contain no loose debris of any kind. An errant screwdriver will never be left inside the cockpit by an errant worker; a stray piece of notepaper will never be allowed inside in the first place; even excess dust is unacceptable, and pad technicians who climb inside a ship will routinely wear protective smocks, booties, and hats to keep such contamination to a minimum. In practice, of course, no anticontaminant precautions are perfect, and something will always be left behind in a spacecraft to attest to the people who have gone before. Generally, that something is small, and it is only when the ship gets to space and gravity looses its hold that the pad-crew mementos in your particular craft will make themselves known. Now, as you arrive in orbit, you're pleased to see that you're flying a reasonably tidy ship. To your right, a single loose bolt somersaults up into the air; to your left, a tiny length of clipped wire spins slowly upward; near the foot of your couch, a bit of loose lint twirls balletically in place. You scoop the bolt and the wire from the air, stow them in a pocket of your pressure suit, and turn to your crewmates with an approving smile.

Having finally arrived in near-Earth space, you've come to a sort of holding room in your voyage to the moon. When Wally Schirra, Donn Eisele, and Walt Cunningham flew up this way aboard Apollo 7, and when Jim McDivitt, Dave Scott, and Rusty Schweickart followed them two missions later aboard Apollo 9, this was as far as they were intended to go. But for every other Apollo mission, commencing with Frank Borman, Jim Lovell, and Bill Anders's Apollo 8, a terrestrial orbit was only the most transient of things. According to the lunar flight plan, a moon-bound crew will spend just under two orbits—or just under three hours—circling the home planet, during which time they will survey their systems, check their equipment, and make sure everything is in order for their journey. Only if all is indeed well will they relight their third-stage engine and head out toward the moon. If the crew discovers a problem before the engine is lit, they will be welcome to try to sort

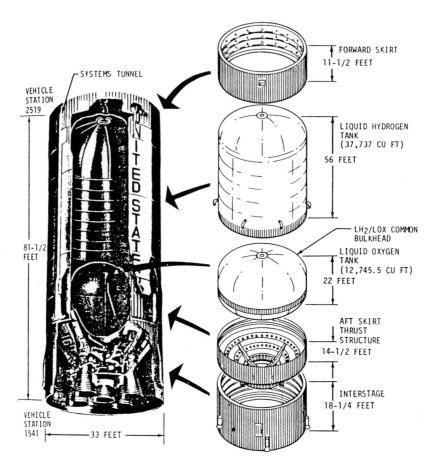

A second-stage tank. (NASA)

it out, but they will only have one additional orbit—or ninety more minutes—to do so. Any longer and the batteries that provide the third-stage booster with power will begin to die. Loss of power in so critical an engine would, of course, spell the loss of the mission, and the crew that had trained for two years to land on the moon would be ordered to return to Earth just a few hours after leaving it.

With so little time to get so much done, and so much riding on doing it well, you don't waste more than a few seconds once you get to orbit reflecting on the fact that you're actually here. The Earth, you know, is rotating panoramically beneath you at a distance of just ten dozen miles, but with the exception of a few stolen glances, you resist the impulse to gaze out your windows and take it all in. As you go resolutely about your business, your spacecraft silently crosses from the daytime side of the Western Hemisphere over to the nighttime side of the Eastern, back to day again and then back to night again with only your faith in orbital physics confirming that this cycling is taking place at all.

When your two allotted circuits come to an end, your ship indeed appears to be functioning smoothly, and the call comes up from the ground that you are, as Houston likes to say, *go for TLI*—or translunar injection. This is the call you've been waiting for, and you and your crewmates exchange a wordless nod, pull yourselves back into your seats, and carefully—with no one else's assistance this time—refasten your restraint harnesses. The TLI maneuver will be a full, five-and-a-half-minute burn of your third-stage engine that will increase your speed from an already blinding 17,500 miles per hour to a near-surreal 25,000.

For several long minutes you wait in your couch while the flight dynamics officers down in Houston double-check your trajectory, and the guidance and navigation engineers take a last look at your gyros, and the environmental and electrical command men run through your power profiles, and the retrofire officers review your emergency procedures, and the flight director, in the middle of the room, polls them all one final time. When he's satisfied that it's safe for you to floor your engine and head away from home, he passes the news on to the capcom, who in turn relays it up to you. At the precise second written into the flight plan a year or two ago, you reach to your instrument panel, relight your third stage, and feel it rumble to life behind your back.

"Burn is go," you might say.

"Pressures look good," one of your crewmates might add.

"Zero degrees yaw," the other might offer.

"Roger," Houston will almost certainly respond.

After those terse exchanges, the air-to-ground loop falls temporarily silent, and you allow yourself a moment to sit back and take stock of your surroundings. With the blackness of translunar space directly ahead of you, your third stage thrumming directly behind you, and your two crewmates sitting silently to your side, you grasp for the first time that you are in fact flying out to the moon. That awareness, you realize, is something NASA could never write into a flight plan.

Earth through the film's frosted lunar-module window.

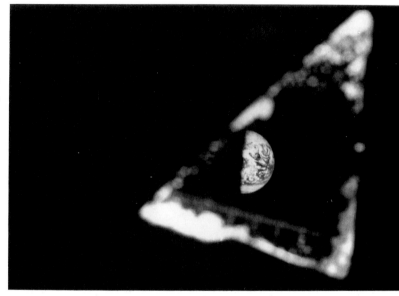

NATIONAL AERONAUTICS AND SPACE ADMINISTRATION
Washington, D.C.

April 18, 1969

Mr. George M. Low
Manager, Apollo Spacecraft Program
NASA Manned Spacecraft Center
Houston, Texas

Dear George:

The recent nicknaming of [the command module and the LEM as] Gumdrop and Spider (Apollo 9) and Charlie Brown and Snoopy (Apollo 10), whether one likes the names or not, brings to mind a situation I'd like to call to your attention. Tom Paine and I have talked about this and perhaps this is a good time—well in advance—to discuss it. The question is: What next for Apollo 11? We feel very strongly that we should have a very careful selection of these kinds of nicknames, and invoke your support to make certain this office knows in advance, before public disclosure, what is proposed. The manned lunar landing mission is, of course, a vital one and one to be witnessed by all mankind— and the appropriateness of nicknames, etc., which may appear casual at one moment is an important matter. I'd appreciate your support and being kept informed as this develops.

Many thanks,

Julian Scheer
Assistant Administrator
for Public Affairs

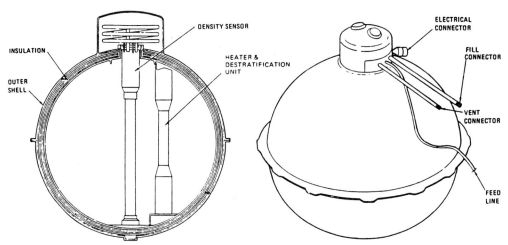

Oxygen cryogenic tank. This is what blew up during the Apollo 13 mission. *(NASA)*

NATIONAL AERONAUTICS AND SPACE ADMINISTRATION
Washington, D.C.

April 19, 1969

MEMORANDUM for: Dr. Mueller
Subject: Symbolic items for the first lunar landing

This is to advise you, the Apollo Program Office, and MSC of the thinking that has emerged from discussions among members of the Symbolic Activities Committee to date on symbolic activities in connection with the first lunar landing.

Further discussions will be necessary prior to the time we make final recommendations. However, in veiw of the general agreement on approach that has been manifested so far, the approach outlined below should be taken as the basis for further planning.

1. Symbolic activities must not, of course, jeopardize crew safety or unduly interfere with or degrade achievement of the mission objectives. They should be simple, in good taste from a worldwide standpoint, and have no commercial implications or overtones.

2. The intended overall impression of the symbolic activities should be to signalize the first lunar landing as an historic forward step for all mankind that has been accomplished by the United States.

3. The "accomplishment of the United States" aspect of the landing should be symbolized primarily by placing and leaving a U.S. flag on the moon in such a way as to make it clear that the flag symbolizes the fact that an effort by American people reached the moon, not that the U.S. is "taking possession" of the moon.

It would be appreciated if any comments, further suggestions, or problems you or others have with respect to the foregoing are made known promptly to me and the committee.

Willis H. Shapley
Associate Deputy Director

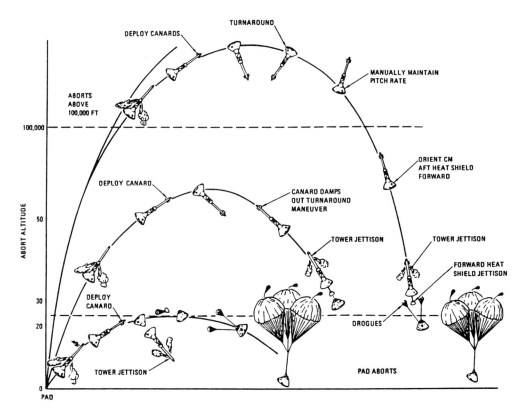

How launch escape subsystem operates at different altitudes.

WESTERN UNION

GENERAL RELEASE
HOUSTON, TEX.

WESTERN UNION ESTIMATES THAT A TOTAL OF 2,500,000 WORDS OF PRESS COPY HAS BEEN HANDLED THROUGH JULY 21, COVERING THE VOYAGE AND MOON LANDING OF APOLLO 11.

ANOTHER 2,000,000 WORDS HAVE BEEN MOVED OVER WESTERN UNION LEASED LINES AND SUBSCRIBER TELEX INSTALLATIONS PROVIDED FOR THE LAUNCH.

MORE THAN 100 OPERATORS, SUPERVISORS, AND TECHNICIANS HAVE STAFFED THE THREE OPERATING ROOMS WHICH HAVE A JOINT CAPACITY OF SOME 250,000 WORDS PER HOUR.

WESTERN UNION

HOX646WUC018 11:29A CDT; JUL.

THOMAS PAINE
NASA, HOUSTON

STILL TIME TO BRING ASTRONAUTS BACK ALIVE, MIRACLE IF THEY MAKE IT
TO MOON, REMEMBER FALL OF ICARUS.

APPREHENSIVELY, E.S., LEXINGTON, MASS

WESTERN UNION

HOX217 FONTANA CALIF 20 3:40 P, PDT

THOMAS PAINE, HEAD OF NASA, CAPE CANAVERAL, FLO

WHY WAS THE NAME OF JOHN F. KENNEDY THE FATHER OF THE BEAUTIFUL
MISSION JUST ACCOMPLISHED OMITTED FROM THE PLAQUE PLACED ON THE
MOON? IT IS ONLY RIGHT THAT THE NAMES OF THE THREE ASTRONAUTS BE
SO PLACED BUT IT IS AN ABSOLUTE AFFRONT TO ALL ON THE PART OF
PRESIDENT NIXON WHO HAD ABSOLUTELY NOTHING TO DO WITH THE
PROJECT TO HAVE HIS NAME PLACED WITHOUT THE NAME OF JOHN F.
KENNEDY.

SINCERELY
R.A., B.F.

WESTERN UNION

HDX728WUC095 TTYO CDT JUL; FORT WORTH TEX

DR. THOMAS PAINE

I WISH TO OBJECT TO THE AMERICAN ASTRONAUTS CARRYING AND PLACING
ON THE MOON THE RUSSIAN ASTRONAUT MEDALS.

O.C., FORT WORTH, TEX

WESTERN UNION

HDX073WUC175 4:26P CDT JUL

THOMAS PAINE, ADMINISTRATOR, NASA

MAY WE SHIP A CHAMPION MASONRY SAW AND DIAMOND BLADE AT NO
CHARGE FOR YOUR USE IN EXAMINING MOON MATERIALS?

A.F.
PRESIDENT, CHAMPION MFG. CO., ST. LOUIS

WESTERN UNION

H0X647 WUC019 11:47A CDT, JUL

DR. PAINE, MISSION CONTROL CTR, HOUSTON

THANKS FOR HAVING MR ALLAWAY RESPOND TO MY LETTER [ABOUT] RADIOACTIVITY DANGER ON MOON SURFACE (STOP) SUGGEST DROPPING SOME METAL OBJECT BEFORE TOUCHING DOWN THE LADDER (STOP) ANY BLAST COULD AFFECT THE FIRING OF THE RETURN ENGINE

S.B., GRAND CONCOURSE, BRONX, NY

WESTERN UNION

HOX079WUC181 5:09P CDT; JUL

DR. THOMAS O. PAINE
NATIONAL AERONAUTICS AND SPACE ADMINISTRATION
HOUSTON

HOW ABOUT NAMING THE MOON "THE LUNAVERSE"?

MISS A.H.
NEW YORK, NY

NATIONAL AERONAUTICS AND SPACE ADMINISTRATION
Washington, D.C.

July 29, 1969

Honorable William H. Marshall
House of Representatives
Washington, D.C.

Dear Mr. Marshall:

This refers to your inquiry on behalf of Mr. Harwood B. Stofer, Cleveland Dowel and Wood Turning Co., concerning any use of wood products in the Apollo 11 spacecraft.

We have asked program officials to look into the matter, and when information is available, we will write you again.

Sincerely,

Robert F. Allnut
Assistant Administrator
Legislative Affairs

6

Re-creating a Moonship

1994, THE FILMING OF *APOLLO 13*

Max Ary, president of the Kansas Cosmosphere and Space Center, is proud of his hole in the ground in Hutchinson, Kansas. It's a big hole—thousands of cubic feet in volume—and it's been getting bigger every day. The tourists who come to Hutchinson don't come to see the hole; even if they *wanted* to see it, Ary has it pretty safely cordoned off. But they do see the building right in front of it. And that building—The Kansas Cosmosphere and Space Center—is worth the trip.

The Kansas Cosmosphere and Space Center has the world's largest collection of space artifacts outside the Smithsonian Institution. Enshrined inside its 50,000 square feet of floor space and exhibit areas are rockets and spacecraft, pressure suits and helmets, tools and equipment and mementos and documents, all chronicling the nearly three and a half decades American astronauts have been traveling in space. Ary, a space-science educator who began his career designing and operating planetariums, began the collection more than twenty years ago, when the Apollo lunar program ended and the contractors who had built

Actor Tom Hanks with astronaut Dave Scott, commander of the Apollo 15 mission.

the hardware that carried human beings to the moon began wondering what to do with the equipment they had left and considered whether it might not be wise simply to break it apart, melt it down, and toss it out. Ary argued it would indeed *not* be wise, raised local funds to build a museum for the machines, and in 1980 founded his Kansas Cosmosphere.

Such a facility in such an unlikely place has become an unlikely success, and with thousands of people traveling to Hutchinson every year to visit the artifacts Ary rescued, the Cosmosphere is now doubling in size, with a 100,000-square-foot hall scheduled to open in 1997 and exhibit not just American space artifacts but Soviet ones as well. That is the reason for Ary's hole in the ground—a hole that should soon be something far more glamorous.

But Max Ary was thinking about more this year than just expanding his Cosmosphere. He was also thinking about making a movie. In March of 1994, director Ron Howard and producer Brian Grazer of Imagine Films decided to bring the tale of the near-disastrous Apollo 13 lunar mission to film. The account of that flight, they knew, was compelling and its dramatic appeal timeless, but just having a good story did not necessarily mean it would be easy to tell it well. The movie *Apollo 13* would be extremely dependent on technology, cutting-edge special effects, and most important, sophisticated sets and props. It would hardly do to make a film in which so much action takes place in Mission Control, for example, without an authentic-looking Mission Control in which to film it. It would hardly do to outfit your actors in what were supposed to be multimillion-dollar pressure suits without mock pressure suits that at least looked like the real things. Most important, it would hardly do to set most of your action inside an Apollo command module and a tiny lunar module without duplicate modules that were indistinguishable from the genuine articles. When it came time to build these two replica ships, Howard and Grazer were told by NASA that Ary was the person they needed.

For Max Ary, building a mock-up Apollo 13 spacecraft was a lot easier than it would be for other space historians—for one very significant reason: he was already in possession of many parts of the real Apollo 13. Like most American spacecraft, the command module *Odyssey,* which served as the cockpit and mother ship for the Apollo 13 mission, had long since been consigned to permanent retirement in a museum in Paris, France. With thirty spacecraft having been flown and recovered in the Mercury, Gemini, and Apollo programs, however, most American museums able to accommodate and care for such an artifact had already received one, and over the years, NASA had begun distributing them to exhibit halls overseas.

Apollo 13—long perceived as America's only failed lunar mission—was a likely candidate for such expatriation, and since the 1970s, the ship had been on display in a science museum in central Paris.

Ary knew, however, that the Apollo 13 module displayed in France was not all there was to the ship. Immediately after splashdown, engineers had disassembled much of the spacecraft to study its construction to determine the cause of the accident that had aborted its mission. When this autopsy was complete, the spacecraft was never fully reassembled, and many of its components—including switches, gauges, knobs, struts, storage cabinets, sections of couches, and even parts of the internal bulkhead—were simply tagged with an Apollo 13 label and stored in NASA warehouses. After the main body of the command module was sent overseas, Ary discovered these bits of the ship and, despairing of ever recovering Apollo 13 itself, claimed at least these small artifacts for his Kansas museum.

Now, Ary believed, these parts of the spacecraft could prove an unexpected windfall. Using this authentic hardware as the core of his reconstruction, and working from extensive blueprints and photographs that had long been part of his collection, he slowly began a ground-up re-creation of a full-scale Apollo spacecraft. Immediately he saw the job would be a big one. To build a command module alone—never mind a LEM—Ary and a team of local engineers would have to manufacture and assemble at least two thousand components, from the largest structural struts down to the smallest lights and toggle switches. Though the genuine Apollo components he did have would give him a bit of a head start on the job, it would only be a small one. Director Howard had already specified that he hoped to have not just one command module built, but two command modules and two lunar modules, plus smaller-scale models of each, allowing filming to take place on more than one set at a time—thus shortening the production schedule. This meant that while Ary might be able to include, say, a real Apollo 13 oxygen gauge in one of his models, he would still have to manufacture at least one or two more for use in the other ships.

Making things even more challenging, Howard had already explained to Ary that the ships he needed would have to differ from the real ones in one significant way: they would have to snap apart and snap back together again. To film in a space as confined as a command module, a director would ordinarily rely on a periscope-like camera that could snake through a small opening in the bulkhead and capture the interior of the ship from numerous different angles. Periscope filming, however, is not always desirable filming, as it limits the number and setups of shots even the most imaginative director could compose.

Howard, known for the wide variety of points of view from which he likes to film, chafed at such limitations. Instead, he (along with production designer Michael Corenblith) preferred a modular command module, with walls, ceilings, and even floors that could swing open and then swing shut again, depending upon the shot he was hoping to compose. To moviemakers, such an access portal for a camera is known as a wilding. To permit the myriad shots Howard envisioned for *Apollo 13,* Ary calculated he would need at least twenty wildings on the command module alone, and then another twenty on the even more cramped lunar module.

For five months, from early spring to midsummer, Ary threw himself into the demanding, Herculean construction project. At a 20,000-square-foot factory where the Kansas Cosmosphere conducts most of its building and restoration work, a staff of forty-five engineers and builders working up to eighty hours per week fabricated and assembled the command module. The spacecraft couches—built from molds cast from authentic Apollo couches—contained nearly four hundred parts each. More than eleven hundred toggle switches—accurate down to the characteristic triangular shape and grip-enhancing ribbing favored by astronauts—had to be ground and milled. The spacecraft hatch—a five-hundred-pound, vaultlike affair containing dozens of cranks, wheels, and cogs—had to be molded from lighter, more affordable plastic, while losing none of the appearance of authenticity. In addition, more than fifteen hundred supplemental items—such as hoses, straps, cameras, dosimeters, flashlights, air filters, and even ink pens—that were not part of the spacecraft but were carried aloft with it had to be copied and manufactured.

During the first eight weeks of the project, the manufacturing went relatively smoothly, and then the production designer, Michael Corenblith, called with a problem. Even with all of the wildings Ary had promised, the command module still appeared too cramped to accommodate three actors, two cameras, and all of the attendant lights and other hardware necessary to compose an effective shot. The crowding was not severe—an additional six inches of elbow room would be all that would be necessary—but it *was* necessary. How easily, Imagine wanted to know, could Ary come up with that additional half foot?

The answer, the designer knew, was *not* easily. Invisibly adding a few extra inches to almost any structure is a reasonably simple matter—unless that structure is a cone. While squares, rectangles, and spheres can grow uniformly at all points, cones do things differently. Expand an area near your apex by two inches, and an area near your base may grow by four or five. Graft on just an eighth of an inch in one spot, and you suddenly find yourself adding two or three somewhere else. Difficult as this is to engineer in an ordinary conical model, it's much more so in a model of a spacecraft, where nearly every millimeter of interior space has to be assigned to hardware or instrument panels or livable space in which the crew can move about. Ary was ultimately able to find and hide the six inches Howard needed, but not without extending at least a couple of his engineers' eighty-hour weeks into ninety- or hundred-hour ones.

At the same time the Apollo 13 command module was under construction, Ary and a number of his engineers set about the task of building a lunar module. This ship, they knew, would present an even greater challenge than the mother ship had. Apollo 13's LEM, like all LEMs, was not designed to return to Earth after its mission, but would instead remain either on the moon or in orbit around it. The Apollo 13 crew, however, without a viable command-service module for the majority of their trip, had to fly their LEM most of the way home. Before reentry, they transferred back to their command module and allowed the spindly craft in which they had hoped to land on the moon to incinerate in the upper atmosphere. Any artifacts from the craft that Ary or other historians could have hoped to recover vaporized with the ship.

Rebuilding this craft for the *Apollo 13* movie thus meant relying exclusively on photographs, blueprints, or examinations of other museum-piece LEMs, built for testing early in the Apollo program but never actually flown.

Despite such lack of source material, the construction of the Apollo 13 LEM went surprisingly smoothly—not least because its interior was shaped less like a problematic cone than an uncomplicated cylinder—and at the beginning of September 1994, Max Ary delivered to Ron Howard a fleet of three command modules and three lunar modules that may not have been suitable for sending three astronauts to the moon, but were certainly up to the job of making three actors *look* as if they were headed there.

For the better part of three months, Tom Hanks, Kevin Bacon, and Bill Paxton lived inside these tiny enclosures, painstakingly re-creating in a

Dean Cundy, the movie's director of photography, in front of the command-module simulator.

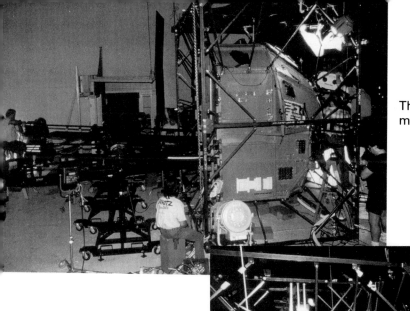

The command-module mock-up.

The command module and the lunar module docked and connected by tunnel.

Tom Hanks in the command-module mock-up.

quarter of a year the ordeal the Apollo 13 crew endured for half a week. But re-creating the interior of the Apollo 13 vehicles for the *Apollo 13* movie was only half the problem. Just as important—and no less challenging—was re-creating the exteriors. For that very different job, Howard and his technical team turned to another group: Digital Domain, Inc., in Santa Monica, California.

In operation for barely three years, Digital Domain is a special-effects company with an impressive cinematic pedigree. Founded by director James Cameron, special-effects designer Stan Winston, and Scott Ross, former head of the special-effects house Industrial Light and Magic, Digital Domain was responsible for the effects in such films as *True Lies* and *Interview with the Vampire,* as well as in numerous commercials and music videos. But none of that experience fully prepared the Digital team for bringing the story of Apollo 13 to life.

The first step for any special-effects crew working on a film as hardware-intensive as *Apollo 13* has always been an obvious one: build models. Stanley Kubrick could not have made *2001: A Space Odyssey* without painstakingly detailed, scaled-down versions of his torus-shaped space station and femurlike Jupiter ship. George Lucas could never have made his *Star Wars* trilogy without equally detailed models of his Millennium Falcon and his Empire Death Star. But what Kubrick and Lucas lacked that later directors like Ron Howard have is computer power—and lots of it.

To generate all of the images needed for *Apollo 13,* Howard and executive producer Todd Hallowell worked with Digital's visual-effects supervisor Rob Legato. They started with a series of storyboards of each shot, and a small fleet of models of the command module *Odyssey* and the lunar module *Aquarius.* Most of the shooting would be conducted with a pair of quarter-scale models, which, when the ships were in their docked configuration, would measure about fourteen feet in length and weigh about eight hundred pounds. In addition, smaller one-twentieth-scale models, measuring less than three feet, would be used for shots that required less detail but more mobility. Finally, there would also be much larger half-scale models of critical, isolated areas of the ship, including the spacecraft panel that exploded into space during the oxygen-tank detonation that destroyed the service module.

All of these models would be filmed the way most space models are—in front of black draping or monochrome screens with cranes and lifts and dollying cameras providing the almost unlimited range of movement the ships

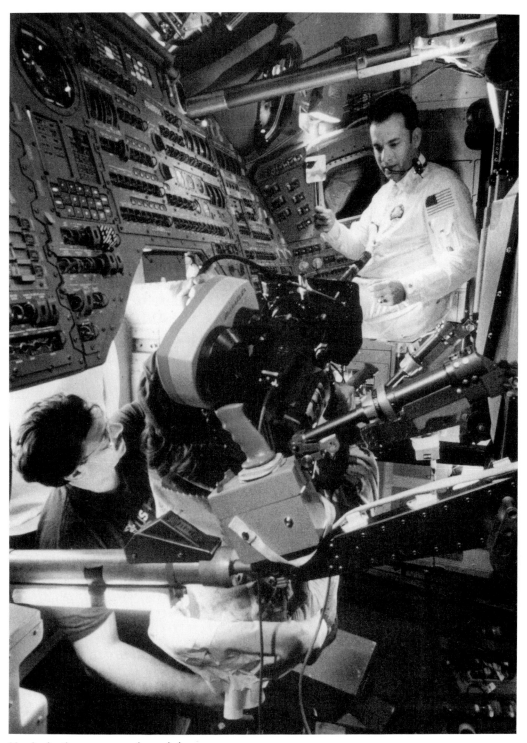
Hanks in the command module.

would exhibit in space. When the film images were converted to video images, reconverted to digital images, and then loaded into computers, however, remarkable things would happen.

The computer systems at Digital Domain are as far above the ordinary PC as rocket ships are above crop dusters. Even for home use, creating and storing pictures and other images requires infinitely more data-processing muscle than simply generating documents or operating spreadsheets. When those images are detailed enough to be included in a major motion picture, the information-crunching requirements are even higher. A single second of screen time requires twenty-four frames of film, each of which demands more than twelve megabytes of processing power and storage space. To create and save the entire second, therefore, would consume more than the entire hard-disk capacity of the average 250-megabyte home computer.

Much of the computing brawn built into the far more powerful systems at Digital Domain has less to do with actually drawing pictures than with manipulating them once they're created. To manufacture the images of Apollo 13's service module exploding, for example, Digital's engineers knew they would need to show sparkling shreds of Mylar insulation blasting away from their aritificial ship exactly as they did from the real ship in translunar space. Drawing the silvery confetti was a simple matter, but how such debris would move when blasted into an environment with no air, no gravity, and an entirely different set of physical laws from those that operate here on Earth was an utter mystery.

With no frame of visual reference to serve as a guide, the Digital engineers instead let their computers do the work. Programming their systems with information about vacuums, gravity, pyrotechnics, rotation rates, and projectile mass, they arranged their digitized Mylar on their screen as it would have been arranged inside the Apollo 13 ship and triggered a data-driven, simulated explosion beneath it. Just what would happen when the explosion took place was anybody's guess, but if the computer understood the physics that had been programmed into it, the Mylar scatter pattern would look like nothing the artists had seen before. The computer, as it turned out, understood perfectly, and as the simulated reflective shreds dispersed across the screen, twinkling in the simulated sun and vanishing into the vastness of space, the engineers knew they had their explosion.

Other spacecraft images were no easier to generate: the streams of smoke— composed of millions of tiny digitized spheres—pouring from the hole the

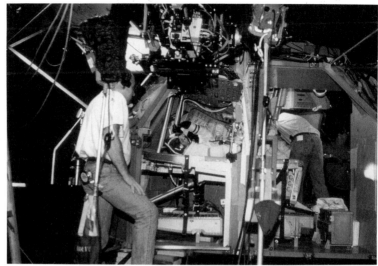

The command-module mock-up during the liftoff scene.

explosion had ripped in the side of the ship; the digitized debris surrounding the service module that had to react with the propellant fired by the ship's thrusters as it drifted into the path of the gas; the tendrils of insulation hanging from the ship, waving not from a breeze in airless space, but from the Newtonian motion imparted by the motion of the ship itself. All of these images had to look authentic, but all also had to obey physical laws alien to the engineers sitting at their earthly computer stations.

As complex as this deep-space footage was to create, however, the film's most impressive effect was a largely terrestrial one: the launch of the Saturn 5 booster that sent the Apollo 13 crew into space and out to the moon in the first place. In order to include this violent, magnificent sequence in the movie, Ron Howard and Rob Legato briefly discussed the possibility of using stock NASA footage. The space agency, after all, had successfully launched ten manned Saturn 5s, each of which was exhaustively documented by film from well before the engines were lit until well after the mammoth, 363-foot rocket disappeared into a flaming speck thirty or forty miles above the ground.

But as Howard quickly discovered, some launches were better chronicled than others, with no single one offering the wide variety of shots necessary to capture the true drama of such an improbable machine leaving the ground. And though every Saturn 5 was essentially indistinguishable from every other Saturn 5, combining all of the launches into one perfect, platonic liftoff was

Tom Hanks and Bill Paxton during the emergency power-up following the accident.

not a realistic option, since each of the boosters left the ground at a different time of day, meaning different lighting conditions that would be at least subliminally evident to even the most untutored audience member.

The answer, of course, was another model—this one an eighteen-foot, one-twentieth-scale rendering of the entire thirty-six-story booster, accurate down to the last star on the last flag painted on its flank. Executive producer and second-unit director Todd Hallowell, it was decided, would then travel to Florida to film the authentic Apollo launch pads and the authentic Canaveral landscapes, then the Digital Domain rocket—filmed on a far less glamorous asphalt lot on the company's Santa Monica grounds—would be superimposed over both. Simulating the launch of the ship would be an equally inelegant matter, with fire-extinguisher exhaust substituting for the liquid-oxygen vapor that shrouds a fully fueled rocket, gunpowder and benzyl peroxide re-

The movie's splashdown and recovery scene. Kevin Bacon is lifted in the rescue basket as Tom Hanks emerges from the spacecraft.

Splashdown and recovery.

creating the hydrogen-and-oxygen explosion that bursts from the first-stage engine bells, and brittle white wax taking the place of the sheets of ice that fall from the booster's sides as it leaves the ground. The film images of this model, too, would then be converted to digital information and loaded into a computer, where it would be made to appear as if it were flying, obeying laws both aesthetic and physical, before it was at last ready to be included in the final *Apollo 13* product.

Notwithstanding all of the respect for visual authenticity that the Digital Domain team brought to the *Apollo 13* project, the visual-effects specialists were not above a bit of playfulness. Last spring, as the final *Apollo 13* images were being completed and polished and readied for shipment to Howard and his editors, Rob Legato and his staff were gathered in a screening room at the company's Santa Monica headquarters for a last critical look. The scene they were inspecting takes place just minutes after the spacecraft explosion, when the crippled *Odyssey* and its attached LEM are bucking through space, while Jim Lovell, the commander, struggles to bring both ships to heel.

As the film began to roll, the screen was filled by nothing but a still, silent star-scape, when the curved bell of the spacecraft's service module engine suddenly slid into view in the lower right-hand corner. Following it was the broad, silver hull of the blast-damaged service module, trailing its cloud of perfectly swirling Mylar and its contrail of microscopically beaded smoke. Following that was the silver cone of the undamaged command module, affixed to the ruined rump of the ship. After the command and service module moved fully into view, the lunar module appeared as well, its crinkly gold skin twinkling in the digitally simulated sun. The twin ships made a quarter turn, faced directly out to space, and began to recede dramatically into the starfield, the LEM's four golden footpads the only part of either ship now directly facing the camera. Before the clip ended, however, the room of silent people watching the image suddenly gaped. Trailing from the forward footpad of the insectile ship was a bright green cartoon frog with a bright red cartoon tongue, struggling heroically to prevent this particular bug from fleeing its sticky grip. The room of computer artists exploded into laughter—Legato most lustily of all.

"That's for the sequel, everybody," he managed to get out. "The *real* secret of the Apollo 13 accident."

7

Mission Control

Sy Liebergot was not equipped to bring Apollo 8 home safely. He knew it; the men sitting around him in Mission Control knew it; even the Apollo 8 astronauts themselves—Frank Borman, Jim Lovell, and Bill Anders—knew it.

If ever there was a bad time for a flight controller like Liebergot to be ill-equipped to bring in his ship, this was it. According to the data on the Mission Control plot boards, the most challenging phase in the most challenging mission in the history of manned space travel was about to get under way. At this moment, the numbers on the screens indicated, Apollo 8 was just a few thousand miles from earth, and speeding toward it—*falling* toward it, actually—at a velocity approaching 25,000 miles per hour. No manned spacecraft had ever traveled anywhere near so fast or anywhere near so far from home. Earlier in the week, so the official log revealed, the Apollo 8 astronauts had become the first human beings to leave the Earth's orbit and visit the neighborhood of the moon, orbiting the rocky body ten times while they observed, mapped, and photographed its surface, con-

Mission Control at the Lyndon B. Johnson Space Center in Houston. *(NASA)*

Mission Control in preparation for launch in the movie *Apollo 13*.

ducting essential topographic surveys for the lunar landing that was scheduled for sometime the next summer. A day later, they had fired their engine and headed for home, and now, so the rapidly dwindling altitude numbers on Liebergot's screen indicated, they were almost there.

For a man in the chair Liebergot was occupying today, a return to Earth by a manned moonship should not have been an inordinately stressful experience. Not that the exercise wasn't a dangerous one; it was. Plunging toward Earth at a velocity approaching 37,000 feet every second, the crew would have to hit the relative brick wall of the atmosphere at an angle that had a margin of error of just 2.5 degrees. If they were too steep, their ship would incinerate like kindling well before it ever hit the ocean; if they were too shallow, it would skip off the top of the atmosphere like a rock skipping off a pond. A reentry of this kind was less a controlled landing than it was a wild high-dive, and nobody responsible for bringing it about safely pretended it was a sure thing.

But happily for Liebergot, as well as for most of the other controllers in the room, the job of pulling off this particular maneuver fell principally on the shoulders of three men: the FIDO, or flight dynamics officer; the GUIDO, or guidance officer; and the RETRO, or retrofire officer. All three sat in the front row of Mission Control—a row appropriately known as The Trench—and though each of the three oversaw different aspects of the mission, all were broadly thought of as trajectory men—the people responsible for plotting the spacecraft's course, orienting its gyros, and generally making sure its aim was true. When you were trying to thread an atmospheric needle like the one Apollo 8 was threading today, your trajectory men were the ones you counted on.

Of course, it wasn't as if the men at the other consoles didn't have anything to do during the upcoming reentry, and Sy Liebergot had more to do than most. Liebergot was working at the EECOM—or environmental and electrical command—console, and as the name implied, his job was to oversee the power and life-support systems of the spacecraft, making sure they continued doing what they needed to do to keep the crew alive and comfortable from liftoff until splashdown. It was no small matter, this business of ensuring the well-being of three astronauts across a quarter of a million miles of translunar void, and in the final hours of the mission, it was a bigger matter than ever. It was at this point, shortly before reentry, that the crew would jettison their service module, the mammoth, cylindrical rear portion of their ship that

Actor Clint Howard as Sy Liebergot.

contained their oxygen tanks, their hydrogen tanks, their power-producing fuel cells, and virtually all of the other hardware that had sustained them for most of the last week. Once this expendable appendage was gone, the crew would have to rely until splashdown on three small batteries and a tiny tank of oxygen built into the conical command module that served both as their living quarters and their reentry pod. If anything went wrong with this modest supply of air and power, the astronauts would quickly perish, expiring in space long before the RETRO, FIDO, and GUIDO could work the navigational magic that would bring the ship home.

Liebergot, though stationed at the EECOM console, was merely an EECOM trainee, one of NASA's backroom engineers still trying out for a spot in the Mission Control auditorium. Seated at the console with Liebergot today—indeed seated practically in front of him—was T. Rodney Loe, a first-string EECOM with a wealth of flight experience in both the Gemini and Apollo programs. Loe would wield the real EECOM authority during Apollo 8's reentry; Loe would call the real shots. Liebergot would merely be doing what was known as *side-saddling*—sharing the EECOM station with his more senior colleague in order to learn the rhythms and the language of the room in which he hoped one day to work on his own.

As the Apollo 8 spacecraft closed in on Earth and the time to discard the service module approached, Liebergot, despite his subordinate status, found himself growing surprisingly nervous. In a few minutes, the order to sever the back end of the Apollo 8 spacecraft would be given, and whether it came from Seymour Liebergot or T. Rodney Loe, it would still be coming from the console they shared. If anything went wrong, they would be sharing the blame as well. If Loe felt the same unease as Liebergot, however, he hardly showed it, studying his monitor, checking his mission clock, and looking about the room with an almost preternatural calm. Liebergot turned to Loe and flashed a tight smile; Loe grinned easily back.

"Say, Sy," Loe said nonchalantly. "You know what I'd like right about now?"

"What's that, Rod?"

"A hot cup of coffee."

"Coffee?"

"Coffee. Sure do have a craving. Can I get you a cup?"

"Uh, Rod," Liebergot said uneasily. "Could it maybe wait awhile? We've got a reentry coming up."

"Heck, Sy. We've still got a few minutes before jettison."

"A few *minutes?*"

"That's all it'll take me to grab a quick cup. You keep an eye on things and I'll be right back."

Liebergot stared confusedly as Loe rose from the console and retreated up the aisle. If any other controllers in Mission Control noticed anything amiss, they didn't show it, and the junior EECOM gaped in wonder as the senior EECOM vanished, unacknowledged, out the door. Casting a glance at the now-vacated chair in front of him, Liebergot edged a little closer to the console monitor, then edged back, then closer, then back again. Finally, he settled on a proximity to the monitor somewhere between where Loe had been sitting and where he, the apprentice, should rightly stay. If any spacecraft systems required the EECOM's attention in the bare minute or two Loe promised he'd be gone, Liebergot would be able to attend to them without feeling he was usurping the position of the man who should have been doing the attending.

But Loe did not return in a minute; and he didn't return in two minutes; and he didn't return in three or four or seven minutes. With the plot board showing the Apollo 8 spacecraft falling toward Earth at a speed of 416 miles *every* minute, it was not long before the time for service-module separation and reentry arrived. Liebergot took one final glance over his shoulder, silently cursed Loe, then hiked his chair all the way up to the console and did the only thing he could do: he okayed the jettison, monitored the numbers while the maneuver took place, and then, satisfied that the spacecraft had indeed shed its hind end without incident, spent the next forty-five minutes helping to bring it through the atmosphere to a safe Pacific splashdown.

When the word came down that Apollo 8 had hit the water successfully, Liebergot fell back in his seat, dropped his head in his hands, and sighed a sigh that was equal parts pride in what he'd just accomplished and shock that he'd been made to accomplish it alone. He was astounded at what Loe had done, and he had half a mind to tell him so. The problem was, Liebergot knew, that no flight director or administrator in all of NASA would agree with him. Given the chance, in fact, the Agency brass would not only not censure Loe for his actions today, they'd probably applaud him for it.

The mission T. Rodney Loe had abandoned so summarily this afternoon was, in fact, not a mission at all. To be sure, Frank Borman, Jim Lovell, and

Mission Control during Apollo 13's final TV broadcast. Gene Kranz (foreground, back to camera) watches Fred Haise on the viewing screen. *(NASA)*

Bill Anders had indeed spent the day in an Apollo spacecraft, but it was a simulated spacecraft bolted to the floor of the crew training quarters just a few hundred yards from Mission Control. The plot board in the control room showed the ship on its way back to Earth after orbiting the moon, but the fact was, Apollo 8's lunar mission was still weeks away. Today's flight was merely a dress rehearsal, designed to drill the men in the spacecraft and the men in the control room in the harrowing business of translunar reentry. Nobody would ever mistake a simulated flight for the real thing, but to a rookie like Liebergot, these make-believe missions had a way of feeling quite real. Today, Rod Loe had decided, he'd make it realer still. As Liebergot, still sitting alone at his console, lifted his head from his hands, he noticed Loe approaching from the back of the room, contentedly sipping his cup of coffee.

"Where the hell were you?" Liebergot asked.

"Getting coffee. Like I said."

"Did it just occur to you to slip off like that?"

"Hell, no."

"You'd *planned* this?"

"Hell, yes."

"And I imagine you think it was clever."

"Don't know; wasn't trying to be clever. Look, Sy, you either get your feet wet in here or you don't get your feet wet. You just did and you did fine. A few weeks from now, when we're flying this thing for real, you're going to remember this and you're going to thank me."

Sy Liebergot ultimately did thank Rod Loe for the training he had given him, just as Rod Loe had once thanked his senior controllers and his senior controllers had once thanked theirs. In the engineering and aerospace community of the early 1960s to the early 1970s, there was no place where the lessons were learned more thoroughly, where the technical protocols were studied more exhaustively, where the wisdom was passed on more thoughtfully, than in the Mission Operations Control Room of the Manned Spacecraft Center in Houston, Texas. Known to the men who worked there simply as the MOCR—rhyming with *poker*—the grand auditorium with its ranks of consoles and gaudy projection screens was one of the most visible symbols of perhaps *the* most visible agency in the scientific world.

In the earliest days of manned space flight, the MOCR was a relatively modest place, mostly because the flights it was designed to oversee were modest as well. When Alan Shepard went aloft for his fifteen-minute ballistic suborbital in 1961, there was no need for an elaborate global tracking network and a MOCR console to monitor it because the spacecraft wouldn't be circling the globe; there was no need for additional spacecraft consoles in Mission Control to oversee additional spacecraft in orbit—a lunar module, for instance, or an unmanned Agena docking vehicle—because no other spacecraft existed. Just flinging Shepard's thimblelike Mercury craft up into space and bringing it down again was accomplishment enough. With such a relatively straightforward mission to oversee, the MOCR could be a pretty spare place, and for Shepard's flight—as well as for the five other missions that followed in the Mercury program—a comparatively modest control room in a building on the grounds of Cape Canaveral in Florida was sufficient to do the job. When the Mercury program ended in 1963, however, all that changed.

The missions NASA planned for its upcoming two-man Gemini ships and its down-the-line three-man Apollo ships were as far beyond the one-man Mercury missions as jet travel was beyond country barnstorming. Envisioned for the future flights were boosters the size of office buildings and spacecraft the size of station wagons, rendezvous in low Earth orbit and dockings in lunar orbit, space walks somewhere in translunar space and hikes on the surface of the moon. For all the new missions and all the new machines to be safely monitored, a new control center would be needed.

In 1962, even before the Mercury program ended, construction began on a far larger, far more sophisticated MOCR in a multibuilding complex halfway across the nation in Houston, Texas. The way the space agency planners envisioned it, the Cape Canaveral space center would continue to be responsible for launching all manned spacecraft, running the show from countdown to ignition to the moment the rocket's engine bells cleared the gantry. After that, the Floridians would pass the baton to the Texans, who would oversee the remainder of the mission, from T plus ten seconds straight through splashdown. While nobody at the Agency disputed the need for a new Mission Control facility, most scratched their heads at the location. To engineers and flight directors who made it their business to know something about the value of keeping systems simple, the idea of bicameral control centers made not a shred of sense. Two centers meant twice as many components to maintain, twice as many men to train, and twice as many things to go wrong. Setting up the new facility so far from Florida, however, had less to do with science than it did with politics.

Well before ground was broken on the new complex, senators and congressmen from around the country knew that the $170-million project would be one of the biggest, fattest, pinkest pieces of pork the government had served up in a long time. NASA's launch pads, the legislators understood, would always have to remain on the safe and relatively remote spits of land on Florida's east coast, but the new control center could be put anywhere. While a lot of politicians lobbied to have the facility placed in their home states, it was only Senate majority leader and legislative mud-wrestler Lyndon Johnson who had the clout, power, and sheer force of will to get the job done. When Johnson, a native Texan, spied the NASA prize, most lesser legislators had the good sense to stand aside and let the majority chief have his way.

Though the entire Manned Spacecraft Center that Johnson had snagged for his constituents was envisioned as a remarkable place, it was the Mission Control auditorium that would be its most remarkable feature. The consoles that filled the room would be arranged in four tiered rows with a half dozen or so stations in each row. In the front left tier were three screens given over to the three men nicknamed Booster 1, Booster 2, and Booster 3. These controllers, as their monikers implied, would oversee the operation of the giant Saturn 5 moon rocket from the moment of liftoff until the moment the astronauts left Earth orbit and began the long coast to the moon. This period spanned barely five or six hours, after which the Booster trio would go home and their consoles would be shut off until the next mission. To the right of the Booster stations, on the other side of an aisle that ran up the center of the room, were the stations of the Boosters' polar opposites: the RETRO, GUIDO, and FIDO, those men whose job it was to steer the spacecraft out to the moon and ultimately bring it home.

In the second row of the MOCR, things became more specialized. Occupying the far left seat in that tier was the flight surgeon, the on-site doctor who monitored the medical data beamed down from the spacecraft and oversaw the health of the crew. Next to the flight surgeon was the capcom, or capsule communicator, the only person during a nominal mission who would speak to the astronauts directly. On the opposite side of the aisle from the capcom was the EECOM, the position that Sy Liebergot was hoping one day to fill. To the right the EECOM were the TELMU and CONTROL stations, where engineers did the same environmental and navigational work for the lunar module that the EECOM, GUIDO, and FIDO did for the command module. Arrayed around the rest of the room were numerous other stations, belonging to various other men—and they *were* exclusively men—including the recovery officer, the Department of Defense officer, the flight activities officer, the instrumentation and communications officer, the network officer, the public affairs officer, and others.

More critical to the operation of the flight than all twenty-three of these stations was a twenty-fourth—a double console near the middle of the third row, belonging to the flight director. The flight director was the unquestioned, unchallenged, undisputed overseer of everything that went on in Mission Control, and though it might be the other controllers who understood the individual systems of the spacecraft best, the flight director alone, on most occasions, fully fathomed the entirety of the mission. So complete was the authority of the MOCR chief that it was even codified in NASA's mission rules: "The Flight Director," the published protocols made clear, "may do anything he feels is necessary for the safety of the crew and the conduct of the flight regardless of mission rules." It was Chris Kraft who drafted that rule in the earliest days of the space agency, and Chris Kraft who, as the first flight director, had benefited most from it. Later flight directors—Gene Kranz, Glynn Lunney, Gerry Griffin, Milt Windler, and others—would exercise the power wisely and well, but none with the same pride of authorship as Kraft.

Membership in so elite a fraternity as the MOCR was not attained easily. All of the controllers awarded a seat in the magnificent auditorium had to overcome considerable obstacles to get there. First of all, they had to work cheap. Mission Control jobs were government jobs, and government jobs, as everyone knew, did not pay well. An engineer applying for a NASA position realized that in the private sector his straight-from-college earning power would be somewhere in the low five figures—a considerable paycheck for a twenty-two-year old in the late 1950s. At the National Aeronautics and Space Administration, the government agency that had just been organized with the purpose of putting human beings in space, the starting salary was just $6,770. Worse, merely being selected as one of the men who would earn these miserly wages was no guarantee that your dream of being assigned to the flight control room would be realized.

Before a candidate MOCR man could be crowned an actual MOCR man, a formidable training gauntlet had to be run—a gauntlet overseen by Chris Kraft. Kraft made it his business to drill and redrill his candidates to within

NASA's lead flight director Gene Kranz. *(NASA)*

Ed Harris as flight director Gene Kranz.

The movie's mission controllers hovering around the Capsule Communicator (capcom) Station.

Gary Sinise as Ken Mattingly in Mission Control.

an inch of their sanity, all with the goal of determining who among the Agency's new recruits had both the technical acumen and the imperturbable calm to oversee a $400-million spacecraft and booster on which three men were depending for their lives. If you were willing to learn from Kraft and, more important, if you were willing to obey Kraft, you had a pretty good chance of staying on with the Agency in some capacity. The only thing short of demonstrable incompetence that could instantly make a new Kraft employee an ex-Kraft employee was dishonesty. If you didn't understand a protocol you were learning, you had to say so. If you screwed up even a small part of a simulation, you had to make it your business to announce your mistake before anyone else announced it for you. This rule applied not only to the comparatively anonymous controllers who would be monitoring the spacecraft during a mission, but also to the charismatic pilots who would be flying it.

One day early in the Mercury program in 1961, Alan Shepard, who had just been chosen to make America's first space flight, flew to Cape Canaveral for a few rounds of simulations with the men in the control room. Even for people accustomed to working with astronauts, Shepard was a glamorous person to have around. But if the flight controllers reacted to the pilot with deference, Kraft was not so dazzled and wasted little time dispatching him to the training room where the Mercury simulator was kept. The make-believe flight got quickly under way and proceeded without incident, until somewhere in the middle of it, Shepard bungled a critical navigation maneuver, a mistake that, in a real spacecraft, could have spelled the loss of the mission. Kraft knew the mistake was the astronaut's, and more important, the astronaut probably knew it, too. For a pilot of such stature to commit an error of such magnitude in front of so large an audience, however, was intolerable, and when Shepard began to discuss the problem, he instantly started explaining it away, placing the responsibility anywhere but on himself. Few people listening in on the conversation were inclined to dispute the charges. This was Alan Shepard, after all. Chris Kraft, however, was not so easily cowed and, after listening for a few moments to the astronaut's explanations, stalked into the simulator room and pulled him into a private corner.

"Alan," he said flatly to the nation's first space hero, "do *not* give me this shit. Tell us what you did and tell us what you didn't do. Don't go covering things up, because we're all supposed to be learning from this thing. All right?"

Shepard, taken aback, allowed as how it was all right, and Kraft, satisfied, let the matter go and let the simulation proceed. If Alan Shepard made another mistake this afternoon, it was likely he'd be owning up to it quickly.

The atmosphere in Mission Control was not always, of course, so grimly disciplined. Indeed, after a training period as grueling as the one through which the candidate flight controllers were put, those who actually made the cut found themselves yielding to occasional moments of playfulness. Now and again, those moments occurred during the flights themselves.

In the hallway outside the Mission Control auditorium, each flight controller was assigned a small locker—little bigger than a shoebox—that was designed to hold that most archetypal emblem of the MOCR member's craft: his headset. On leaving work at the end of his shift, a controller would lock his headset away for the night and, at the beginning of the next shift, reclaim it. The lockers—four dozen in all—were arranged six tall and eight wide along a wall, and though none of the tiny doors was labeled with anyone's name, all of them were numbered, making finding your own a simple matter. Late in the training period for the 1971 Apollo 14 flight—the third lunar landing and another Al Shepard mission—Sy Liebergot was retrieving his headset at the beginning of his shift when he noticed, a few lockers away, a red, embossed label affixed to one of the little doors.

CAPCOM LOCKER, the embossed letters said.

Liebergot stared at the label and laughed to himself. Though four rotating capcoms were working this mission, he knew that this just *had* to be the work of Bruce McCandless. McCandless was a member of one of the most recent astronaut classes, and though he was training hard for the Apollo program, he realized that he would probably not get the chance to fly until the Skylab or shuttle programs still some years away. Nevertheless, he worked stubbornly at his lunar flight training—and indeed, at virtually everything he did at NASA. Bruce McCandless studying to be a capcom pushed himself to be the best possible capcom; Bruce McCandless training to be a backup pilot pushed himself to be such a good one that the Agency would be sorry it couldn't fly him in the prime crew member's place. Worrying about whether he could identify a locker that was easy to identify already was exactly the kind of detail McCandless would concern himself with, and solving the problem with a red, embossed label was exactly his kind of solution.

Liebergot nodded his head amusedly and made his way to his console in the MOCR. The EECOM station was directly across the aisle from the

Hollywood mission controllers during the Apollo 13 crisis.

capcom's, and as Liebergot was settling into his seat, he looked to his left and noticed that McCandless was already on duty and already talking earnestly on the communications loop. Taking a second look at the capcom, Liebergot immediately had to turn and stifle a laugh. On the talk-and-listen switch on McCandless's headset were two additional labels, reading, appropriately enough, TALK and LISTEN. On the telephone built into the console was yet another label, which read CAPCOM TELEPHONE. Liebergot nudged the guidance and navigation officer sitting to his right, gestured to McCandless, and the controller responded with a laugh and a shrug.

Little more than a week later, when Apollo 14 had been launched and Al Shepard, Stu Roosa, and Ed Mitchell were on their way to the moon, Bruce McCandless arrived at Mission Control to begin his shift. Approaching the wall of lockers, he quickly scanned for the familiar red CAPCOM LOCKER label and his eye immediately fell on it. On the locker next to the one he assumed was his, however, he was surprised to see another red sticker positioned exactly as his was and reading—exactly like his—CAPCOM LOCKER. On the locker adjacent to that one, he saw another red sticker, and another on the next one and another on the one next to that. Indeed, on every one of the forty-eight lockers—six high and eight wide—was a neatly applied, bright red capcom label. If this was someone's idea of a joke, it certainly wasn't funny. There was work to be done inside the MOCR, and McCandless didn't have time to be fooling about with a lot of now-indistinguishable locker doors, looking for the one that was his.

After a few moments, the capcom did locate his own locker, retrieved his headset, and began to make his way into Mission Control. Before he could set foot inside, however, he was brought up short by something on the doorjamb: another red sticker. This one read THIS WAY TO CAPCOM CONSOLE. Arriving at the console itself, McCandless noticed still more red labels. CAPCOM CHAIR said the one on his chair. CAPCOM MONITOR said the one on his monitor. CAPCOM LEFT ARMREST and CAPCOM RIGHT ARMREST read the ones on his left and right armrests.

If Bruce McCandless—rookie astronaut, rookie capcom, veteran workhorse—was amused, he did a heroic job of not showing it, and as he looked around the room, it was clear that the men in Mission Control, one of whom was obviously behind this, were studiedly revealing nothing either. McCandless sat down at his console, clicked onto the air, and hailed the spacecraft to alert the crew that a new capcom was on duty.

"Apollo 14, Houston," he called out in the requisite uninflected tones of Mission Control.

"Hey, Bruce," Al Shepard called down from thousands of miles away in translunar space. "Good to hear your voice. Have any trouble finding your headset today?"

For an instant, nobody in the MOCR responded—and then every man at every console, including Bruce McCandless, broke into laughter. Off to the right, McCandless couldn't help but notice, Sy Liebergot was laughing loudest of all.

Ron Howard directing in the movie's painstakingly constructed Mission Control.

8

Hollywood Mission Control

1994, CALIFORNIA

Gerry Griffin was accustomed to being in Mission Control. The former Apollo-program flight director was used to the look of the room, the feel of the room, the shadowless whitewash of lighting that poured down from the recessed fluorescents that illuminated the room. He knew without looking what color the flight-controller consoles would be—a pale institutional green. He knew without asking what the wallpaper would be like—a yellow-brown earth tone with a nubby, plasticky finish. He knew without glancing upward the very configuration of the acoustical tiles in the huge drop ceiling—a square-rectangle-rectangle, square-rectangle-rectangle pattern repeated over and over again.

Griffin had spent some of the most remarkable years of his professional life in the big, thrilling auditorium, and the layout of the place was not something he would easily forget. Today, however, when he walked into the silent room with its rows of blinking consoles, something was radically different. The Mission Operations Control Room—known as the MOCR to the men who worked there and as Mission Control to the public—had been located for three decades in Building 30 at the Manned Spacecraft Center in Houston, Texas. Today, however, Gerry Griffin found his MOCR on Stage 27 at Universal Studios in Los Angeles, California.

Four months ago, in April 1994, Griffin had learned that the moviemakers at Imagine Films along with those at Universal had decided to bring the story of Apollo 13 to the screen. One of the first steps in making that ambitious plan a reality was to build a replica Mission Control in which some of the movie's most dramatic scenes—those in which a few dozen young flight controllers conduct their round-the-clock efforts to bring the crippled Apollo 13 spacecraft home—could be filmed. Just a few days ago, construction had been completed on that mammoth set, the actors playing the flight controllers had been cast, and Griffin, along with Jerry Bostick, another Mission Control veteran, had been asked here to spend the first month of filming serving as on-site consultants and resident experts on the ways of the MOCR. Their first job upon arriving today would be to conduct a sort of total-immersion Mission Control school, in which the thirty-six newly cast performers would learn as much as they could about the work done by the men they would spend the next four weeks portraying.

Hollywood Mission Control during a shift change.

Griffin, Bostick, and the actors weren't the only people here today. Also on hand was Jim Lovell, commander of the Apollo 13 mission; Michael Bostick, the son of Jerry Bostick and an Imagine Films vice president, one of the people who had lobbied hardest on behalf of the film in the first place; and Ron Howard, director of *Apollo 13,* who was even more anxious than his actors to hear what Griffin and the senior Bostick had to say today. The two mission controllers wasted no time in getting started, and when they did, the first thing they wanted to discuss was the set itself.

"On the whole, the room looks terrific," Griffin said, "especially the consoles."

"Terrific," Bostick agreed.

"But you want to watch out for some of those warning lights. You've got too many of them blinking. A few is fine, but you'd never have so many going at once."

Howard nodded and made a note.

"And the ones that *are* blinking," Bostick added, "shouldn't all be synchronized the way they are. Throw off the rhythm a little. Nothing gives away a fake console more than having all the lights flashing at once."

Howard wrote this down, too.

"Another important thing," Griffin said. "You're going to need some ashtrays at those consoles. This mission was flown in 1970; *everybody* smoked then."

Howard nodded to his prop master, Steve Levine, who wrote "ashtrays" in his notebook.

The discussion went on for a few more minutes, with Bostick and Griffin pointing out other details—too small perhaps for the audience to see, but not too small for the filmmakers to address—and Howard or a member of his technical crew making note of them. Before long, however, the topic turned to the real focus of the meeting: the flight controllers who once worked in Mission Control and the actors who would be portraying them now. For the next several hours, Bostick, Griffin, and Lovell regaled the room with stories of the eleven Apollo missions—and Apollo 13 in particular—as well as details about the men who ran those missions on the ground. The questions from the actors were numerous and insightful.

"What was the difference," someone wanted to know, "between a guidance officer and a guidance, navigation, and control officer?"

Bostick nodded at the question—a not unexpected one—and explained that

Author Jeff Kluger with Mission
Control veteran Gerry Griffin on
the set of *Apollo 13.*

Technical advisers Gerry Griffin
and Jerry Bostick in Mission
Control.

one of the controllers was responsible for planning spacecraft trajectories, while the other one dealt with the hardware that helped maintain those trajectories.

"Was it ever permissible," another actor asked, "for a controller to talk directly to the astronauts in the spacecraft?"

"Never," Griffin answered. "The flight controllers relayed any technical information to the flight director, who in turn relayed it the capcom—or capsule communicator. He then relayed it up to the ship."

"Who was the final authority in Mission Control during a flight?" a third actor asked.

"Technically, the NASA administrators in the fourth row of consoles were the highest-ranking people present in the room," Bostick answered, "but it was the flight director in the third row who was the true boss of the mission."

"During a crisis like Apollo 13," a fourth person asked, "would flight controllers stay at the space center around the clock or would they go home at the end of the day?"

"Depended on where you lived," Griffin said. "If your house was close by, you tried to get home for a few hours at least, if only to change your clothes and take a shower. Personally"—Griffin gestured beyond the west wall of the Mission Control room he knew so well—"I lived just a mile or so out that way." No sooner had Griffin said this than he caught himself, laughed, and looked around at the familiar auditorium.

"Actually, I didn't," he said with a smile. "Out that way is Los Angeles. I lived in Houston. I'm going to have to keep reminding myself of that."

In the spring of 1994, when Ron Howard and Brian Grazer decided to produce *Apollo 13,* one of the first things they did was to contact the folks at NASA. It would be impossible, the filmmakers knew, to make a credible movie about one of the space agency's most dramatic missions without getting the physical details of both the sets and costumes exactly right—and it would be impossible to do that without the cooperation of NASA. Happily, the space agency was willing to lend a hand.

Though much of the public had long viewed Apollo 13 as one of the country's three great space disasters—less catastrophic than the Apollo 1 fire and the Challenger explosion, perhaps, but only because the Apollo 13 crew survived—much of the space community saw it differently. If the United States hoped to become a space-faring nation, they reasoned, it would have to learn how to cope with the unexpected—and Apollo 13 proved that it could. The press and the public rarely discussed that side of the story, but if someone was thinking of making a feature film that just might tell it now, the space agency would be happy to lend its help.

One of the first things NASA offered the filmmakers was, unexpectedly, the use of Mission Control itself. Only a few months before Howard intended to begin shooting, NASA was to retire the MOCR auditorium in which the flight of Apollo 13 had been run. For the last thirteen years, that room had been one of two used to oversee the missions of the nation's fleet of space shuttles, but with the technology of the 1990s fast outpacing the speed at which a room from the 1960s could be upgraded, NASA planners had decided to mothball it and build a new Mission Control. Would Howard, they wanted to know, be interested in bringing his crew to Houston and directing his MOCR scenes in this historic auditorium itself?

Howard was grateful for the offer, but he knew he had to turn it down. Filming *Apollo 13*'s Mission Control scenes at the Manned Spacecraft Center would mean transporting dozens of actors, dozens of members of the technical crew, and truckloads of equipment, costumes, and cameras to Houston, then

Ed Harris in Mission Control watching the Apollo 13 coverage.

The film astronauts' families and the NASA PR director in the VIP room watching the broadcast from space.

setting up camp there for more than a month. That kind of hemi-continental migration, of course, would mean not only a breathtaking expenditure of labor, but also a breathtaking expenditure of funds. Moreover, once the crew was set up in Mission Control, the remarkable room might not lend itself to filming. To compose some of the shots Howard envisioned, dolly tracks would have to be laid around the floor of Mission Control, often exactly where flight-controller stations currently stood. Installing the rails would mean pulling out the consoles and then reinstalling them later, something even the cooperative NASA would no doubt frown upon. Other possible shots could only be captured with an overhead crane—a piece of equipment that's easy to accommodate on a Hollywood set where the ceiling can be snapped on and off like the lid of a jar, but not so easy to accommodate in a government building with a fixed acoustical ceiling and a steel-and-concrete roof. Tampering with the room's overhead structure would be even more difficult than tampering with its consoles and would also not please the space agency.

Given these drawbacks, Howard and Grazer wisely declined NASA's generous offer and built a modular Mission Control of their own right on a stage at Universal Studios. To get this job done, the director and producer hired an unusually gifted cinematic architect, Michael Corenblith.

Corenblith is a production designer in both film and television who had previously worked on numerous movies including *Cool World* and *He Said, She Said;* he had won an Emmy Award for outstanding production design for the 1983 Academy Awards show. If there is one lesson he or any other production designer learns from such complex projects, it's that in designing a set, you don't draw so much as a single blueprint or drive so much as a single nail until you're completely sure of what it is you're trying to build.

The first thing Corenblith did after being hired was to travel to Houston to explore the real Mission Control. During several visits to the space center, he and his five-person design team shot more than five hundred rolls of film and drew up more than thirty pages of blueprints. When they returned to Los Angeles and sat down with their construction team, they knew they had their work cut out for them. The real Mission Control, they explained to the builders, was more than fifteen feet tall from carpet to ceiling and included more than 8,000 square feet of floor space. The replica Mission Control would have to be built not on any studio stage, but on Universal's Stage 27—one of the largest in Hollywood—covering it from one end to the other, from fire line to fire line. More than 7,200 square feet of recyclable lumber would be needed—enough to build three single-family ranch houses from the cellar up.

Once the shell of the MOCR was built, it would have to be filled with props, hardware, and set dressings unlike any Corenblith had ever assembled before. More than two dozen individual consoles would contain forty-five working monitors and thousands of lights, switches, and knobs; attached to the consoles would be vintage pneumatic tubes that 1970 flight controllers relied upon to send documents back and forth to one another; in the front of the room would be a six-hundred-square-foot projection screen that the real mission controllers

The actresses playing the Lovell daughters (at left, Emily Ann Lloyd; at right, Mary Kate Schellhardt) on the set of the Lovell home.

used to display data, track their spacecraft, and watch live broadcasts from the inside of the cockpit or the surface of the moon; the chairs, tables, bookshelves, coatracks, clipboards, notebooks—all would have to be identical to the kinds manufacturers built and the government bought more than a generation ago.

As Corenblith and set decorator Merideth Boswell contemplated the details of the room, the two decided to attempt a level of historical accuracy that approached archival correctness. If it was only a little harder to fill a room with technically accurate props than with technically inaccurate ones, why not be true to history? For that reason, when Corenblith and Boswell discovered the kind of wallpapers used in Mission Control had long since been discontinued, they found the closest type they could, then added a subtle glaze to make it closer still. When they discovered that the carpet that was fashionable in 1970 was not readily available now, they kept looking until they found an obscure supplier who had just enough square feet to fill the room. For the flight controllers' consoles, they found vintage Mission Control pens, and vintage 1970 slide rules.

When Boswell's research revealed that the men in the front row of Mission Control had had matchbooks printed up with the nickname "The Trench" stamped proudly on the cover, she had identical matchbooks made up for her Trench, too. When Boswell and Corenblith discovered that real mission controllers had equipped each of their consoles with a box of pencils sharpened to daggerlike points, ripped the top off the box and taped it to the consoles so that a fresh pencil could be pulled out whenever it was needed like an arrow being pulled from a quiver, prop pencils and prop boxes were prepared in the same way and carefully attached to each of the prop consoles.

By the time the Mission Control set was finally built, Corenblith could count only three details in the entire room that distinguished the replica MOCR from the genuine article. Each console was equipped with a small gooseneck reading lamp to provide the cinematographer with spot illumination he might need for close-ups; the VIP gallery at the back of the auditorium was equipped with six medium-size viewing windows instead of three large ones because the oversize panes of glass simply weighed too much to be supported in their frames; and the front left corner of the room near the viewing screen veered to the left by an extra inch, a concession necessary to accommodate a load-bearing beam.

Apart from those liberties, the *Apollo 13* production crew built a dead-on,

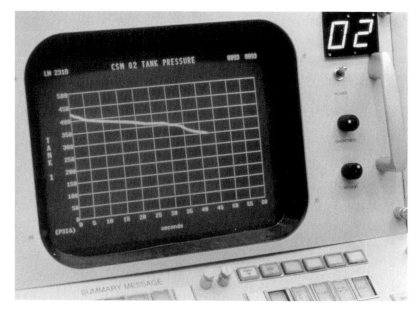

Oxygen tank #1 begins to fail early in the movie.

museum-piece MOCR—and they did so in less than six weeks' time. Only when they were finished would the true work that had to be done in the room get underway.

When, on August 15, 1994, filming began in *Apollo 13*'s Mission Control on Stage 27, most people realized the shoot would not be easy. As in the real Mission Control, dozens of people would be moving through the room at any given moment, and Ron Howard knew that all of them would have to be incorporated—practically choreographed—into even the most intimate shots. What's more, not only would people be walking and working in Mission Control, they would also be talking. During an ordinary lunar mission, the MOCR was filled with a constant, low-level conversational buzz, as controllers conferred with the men on either side of them, murmured into their headsets to their support teams in the back room, or hailed the flight director on the room's closed communications loop.

To make this unbroken background babble as accurate as possible, Howard asked Bostick and Griffin to sit down with all of the Mission Control actors and fill them in on what the men at their particular stations would have been concerned with at any given point in the mission and the phrasing they would have used. In addition, the actors were encouraged to find out who their real-life counterparts were during the Apollo 13 mission and contact them to fill in any additional details Bostick and Griffin couldn't.

Getting the background dialogue right was more than passingly important. When filming got under way, Howard planned to equip all of his actors with live microphones so that their extemporaneous conversations could be preserved and included in the film when a few seconds of technical chatter were needed.

Making the planned filming even more of a challenge was the segmented way in which the *Apollo 13* screenplay had to be shot. Virtually all of the scenes in Mission Control occur after the spacecraft has been launched and the crew is flying either out to the moon or back toward Earth. Many of the most dramatic exchanges in the MOCR, therefore, take place not between controllers conversing face-to-face in the room, but between controllers and astronauts conversing long distance on the air-to-ground loop that connected the MOCR and the ship. Since the Mission Control scenes, however, were the first ones filmed, no communications were coming down from the ship, so no conversations could really be held.

In most movies, a problem like this is solved simply by having a random actor or extra sit off-camera while a scene is being filmed and drone back dialogue to which the on-camera actors can respond. Later, after the corresponding scene is shot with the real actors, the two sets of film can be spliced together and the illusion of an authentic conversation can be created.

In *Apollo 13,* no such substitute actors would be needed—at least not in the MOCR. With Tom Hanks, Kevin Bacon, and Bill Paxton still a month away from shooting any of their scenes, the three actors had nevertheless begun spending more and more time on the Mission Control set, getting to know the people who would be playing the controllers and familiarizing themselves with the atmosphere of the room. When the time came to film scenes that included air-to-ground dialogue, it seemed pointless to have three stand-ins read the lines that the three leads would eventually be speaking anyway. Instead, Hanks, Bacon, and Paxton, who, technically, were not even expected to be working yet, began reporting to work with the rest of the performers, donning headsets, and vanishing into a back room where they could transmit their air-to-ground dialogue in the same heard-but-not-seen way as authentic lunar pilots transmitting from their ship.

On occasion, the reading of this dialogue became a bit more complicated. Early in the Mission Control shooting schedule, Howard was filming a scene

The film's Mission Control during splashdown.

in which the Apollo 13 crew are on-camera broadcasting a television show down to Earth while the flight controllers at their consoles and the astronauts' families in the VIP gallery watch them on the viewing screen at the front of the room. This, of course, required more than simply having the three stars read their lines off-camera, since the people in Mission Control had to be reacting not only to the astronauts' voices, but also to their images on the screen.

With no such images yet available, however, Hanks provided the next best thing, emerging from the back room and scaling a nine-foot ladder in front of the MOCR's viewing screen where, wearing an unspacemanlike plaid shirt and baggy khaki shorts, he recited the dialogue he would eventually be seen delivering on the screen.

For much of the morning, the filming went well, with Hanks as Jim Lovell explaining how astronauts take care of ordinary housekeeping chores in space, including tidying up their cockpit and making dinner.

"An astronaut needs to be his own short-order cook," he would say. "Of course, in zero gravity we don't so much make dinner as just add hot water. Fred Haise is going to be the first person to eat grits in space, and from the look of that food packet, he's also going to be the last."

For the first few hours of filming, all the actors in Mission Control reacted believably to this monologue, treating each reading as if it were the first time they had heard it. Shortly before lunch, however, Howard could see that the child actors in the viewing gallery, who were playing the astronauts' sons and daughters, were starting to get fidgety, and the desired combination of true delight and vague embarrassment they were supposed to be feeling as they watched their fathers on worldwide TV was beginning to look like something closer to disinterest. Mary Kate Schellhardt, the oldest of these performers and one of the stars of *Free Willy II,* was doing a better job than most of holding character, and even she was beginning to fade. After a few less-than-energetic takes, Howard called Hanks down from his perch.

"We're starting to lose the kids," the director said to his actor. "They look more than a little bored."

"I don't blame them," Hanks said. "They've heard me do this thing about a hundred times."

"Want to see if you can vary it some? Maybe stir them up a little?"

Hanks thought for a moment, then smiled. "No problem," he said, and climbed back up his ladder. When Howard yelled, "Action!" the actor resumed his work, reciting the dialogue he had been reciting since eight o'clock that morning.

"An astronaut needs to be his own short-order cook," he began yet again. "Of course, in zero gravity we don't so much make dinner as just add hot water. Fred Haise is going to be the first person to eat grits in space, and from the look of that food packet . . . from the look of that food packet . . ." Hanks blanched a little and affected a look of confusion and horror. "Wait a minute. That's not grits! That's . . . that's . . . *whale!* Oh, no! It's a Free Willy sandwich!"

Up in the VIP gallery, Mary Kate Schellhardt began to laugh and, then, ever the professional, looked down at her hands and suppressed her welling amusement into the barest smile—exactly as a teenage girl would if she was experiencing a combination of true delight and vague embarrassment while watching her father on worldwide TV. With a broad smile, Ron Howard called "Cut," Tom Hanks climbed back down from his ladder, and the Mission Control crew broke for lunch.

Three months after the *Apollo 13* shoot ended, Michael Corenblith was on a stage at Twentieth Century–Fox, working on his next film, an underwater feature called *Down Periscope.* Once again he would be building a technology

Ed Harris and Mission Control celebrating after the splashdown.

heavy set; once again he would be using the hardware of one era in a film being made in another; and once again he would be trying to do both with as uncompromising an eye for accuracy as possible.

Today, however, his mind was not on the set he was designing for his current movie, but on the one he had built for his last one. Mission Control had been the focus of the *Apollo 13* crew's activity for the initial month of the shoot, but as the first set to be used in the movie, it was also the first set to outlive its usefulness. In Hollywood, where stages are in constant demand and where the cost of tying one up can be high, a set that has outlived its usefulness doesn't last long. Barely a day after the final frame was shot in the

Tom Hanks being photographed in the simulated command module.

Jim Lovell being suited up a few hours before the launch of Apollo 13 on April 11, 1970. (NASA)

The Vomit Comet, otherwise known as the KC-135 weightlessness simulator, on its parabolic course. (NASA)

The Apollo 13 Saturn 5 on the launchpad. (NASA)

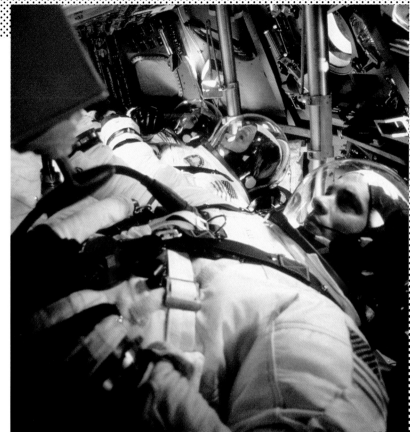

The *Apollo 13* crew during liftoff. From left to right: Bill Paxton, Kevin Bacon, and Tom Hanks.

The crew during a later stage of liftoff. The spacecraft has begun to pitch forward.

In their LEM, Haise and Lovell (Paxton and Hanks) discuss their decaying trajectory with Mission Control in Houston.

Ed Harris as Gene Kranz in Mission Control.

During the film, Tom Hanks as Jim Lovell dreams of the lunar walk he would never take.

Bill Paxton as Fred Haise on his way back to Earth. Haise was about to spike a fever of 104 degrees.

The movie crew struggles to keep the command module stable shortly after the accident.

Houston Mission Control on April 17, 1970: the controllers watch splashdown and recovery on the viewing screen. (NASA)

The movie's Mission Control.

The movie's command module shortly after splashdown.

Ron Howard directing the splashdown scene in *Apollo 13.*

Digital Domain
special effects.

MOCR, *Apollo 13* technicians arrived and began dismantling the remarkable room. The loose furniture went first, followed by the fixed consoles, followed by the carpet and the windows and the ceiling tiles and the wallpaper and then, finally, the walls themselves. Within a week, the set was gone, the vast concrete floor of the stage was swabbed, and another film crew with other blueprints had moved in and begun building.

Corenblith had not been there to watch his MOCR get dismantled—just as he had avoided being there when most of his other sets were reduced to cinematic rubble. It's a prerogative, he figures, of a production designer to be absent when one of his constructions comes down, just as it's a responsibility to be there when it goes up. But it's more than avoidance that helps a person who does what Corenblith does for a living deal with the impermanence of his work; it's a sense of perspective, too—a perspective that even today, months after Mission Control was razed, he must occasionally remind himself to maintain.

"Movie sets, like any other work of architecture, are built to have a very specific life," he says. "But unlike a house, which lives its life on a suburban street, or an office building, which lives its on a city street, a movie set lives only on film. It's not always easy when something you've worked so hard to build is torn down so quickly. The consolation is, once it's committed to celluloid, it can live there forever."

Kevin Bacon as Jack Swigert.

9

Astronaut Talk

"First time I ever felt warm about the dark."
—John Young

You've always respected a lot of things about Neil Armstrong, but his verbal skills were never among them.

When it came to flying, of course, Neil was perhaps the best pure pilot the Agency had; you knew it, your fellow astronauts knew it, even Armstrong himself, you suspected, knew it. It was Neil, after all, who brought his Gemini 8 spacecraft to heel when it spun out of control 120 miles above Earth, threatening the lives of himself and his junior pilot, Dave Scott, just a few hours into what was supposed to have been the most ambitious mission to date in the young Gemini program. It was Neil who had the icy calm and the trip-wire reflexes to bail out of that Lunar Landing Training Vehicle when it was heading for a crack-up on the tarmac at Ellington Air Force Base. Most impressive, it was Neil who had the imperturbability to bring a real LEM, the now-historic *Eagle,* to rest in the soil of the Sea of Tranquillity after low fuel and an overloaded computer nearly turned the first lunar landing into a mere wave-off. If you were in the market for an almost inhumanly good pilot, Neil Armstrong was clearly the man you were looking for. If you were looking for a poet, however, you might look somewhere else.

Certainly, Armstrong never went looking for a job in which a talent for lyricism was required, and nobody who ever hired him expected anything of the kind. In late 1968, however, when it was announced that Neil A. Armstrong, a thirty-eight-year-old Ohio test pilot, would likely become the first human being to set foot on the moon, his ability to mark the moment with an elegantly turned phrase became a matter of national—if not global—interest.

Until very late in the game, of course, it was never a sure thing that Armstrong would be tapped for the honor that every astronaut in the NASA corps coveted. First of all, it was never a sure thing that Apollo 11, the mission for which Armstrong was named commander, would land on the moon at all. Four earlier Apollo missions had to come off perfectly before Agency planners would have enough confidence to commit a crew to an actual touchdown on the moon. If anything significant went wrong on any of those flights, the first landing could be pushed back to Apollo 12 or 13 or 14, bestowing the first moonwalker honors on Pete Conrad or Alan Shepard or Jim Lovell.

Moreover, even when it did become clear that Apollo 11 would get the first shot at the first landing, it was by no means clear that Armstrong would be the first one down the ladder. Up until now, whenever an astronaut had ventured outside his spacecraft, it was always the junior pilot who got the job—and with good reason. Since it was the commander's presumably superior piloting skills that earned him the senior slot in the first place, it was considered prudent to keep him inside the ship and in front of the controls at all times, the better to handle any emergency that might come up while his junior pilot frolicked in the void. Though a lunar landing would be a very different business—not least because both astronauts would be venturing onto the surface—tradition, superstition, and a pilot's taste for the natural order of things argued in favor of the commander staying inside and tending to his ship for as long a time as possible.

But orderliness was not the only consideration in this case; history was, too. And both Neil Armstrong and his copilot, Buzz Aldrin, hoped to make it. The most important factor weighing in Armstrong's favor was that he simply *wanted* to be the first of the two men on the moon. The usual rule requiring the junior pilot to leave the spacecraft before the skipper was not a hard-and-fast one—certainly not as hard-and-fast as the rule that the commander was the final arbiter of anything that happened aboard his ship. If Neil Armstrong decided to change the order of crew egress for the most momentous of all space missions, nobody was willing to do much to challenge him.

Just as important was the fact that Armstrong, unlike Aldrin and most of the other men in the astronaut corps, was a civilian. For the last year, ever since it had become clear that the United States was going to beat the Soviet Union to the moon, the NASA Public Affairs Office had been working overtime to assure a Cold War–weary world that the landing would be peaceful. No territorial claims would be made in the Sea of Tranquillity; no military or surveillance hardware would be carried aloft by the crew; indeed, no political ramifications of any kind would be associated with the trip. With the exception of an American flag that would be planted in the lunar soil as a mere ceremonial formality, the mission that was being flown that week could have been dispatched by virtually any country on Earth. So sensitive was NASA to the concerns of the rest of the world that when the first version of the official mission patch was submitted—showing a bald eagle landing majestically on the moon's surface—it was rejected and returned to the artist for modifications. The eagle's talons, it was felt, looked too clawlike, too subliminally threatening, as if they were preparing to gouge a divot from the lunar soil. In the final, approved version, an olive branch was inserted into the talons, making it clear that this particular bird of prey had something other than predation on its mind. If a stitched eagle on a cloth patch had the rest of the global community feeling skittish, a career military man climbing down the lunar ladder for humanity's first step on a new world would trouble it tenfold. Armstrong, a civilian pilot, should solve that problem neatly.

More than politics and Neil Armstrong's primacy as commander, however, had to be considered in deciding who would be first on the moon. There were also the considerable talents of Buzz Aldrin. Aldrin had flown in space once before—aboard Gemini 12 with Jim Lovell, in 1966—and as second-in-command of that two-man craft, he had set a record for spacewalking that still stood, spending nearly five and a half hours outside his tiny ship. If anyone had earned a reputation for outside-the-spacecraft grace, it was Aldrin, and when the second-in-command slot was being filled for the first lunar landing, this at least appeared to be one of the flight planners' key considerations.

To send your most gifted space walker aloft on your most ambitious mission and then limit, by even a few minutes, the time he would walk made little sense to an organization as risk-averse as NASA—and it certainly made little sense to Aldrin. No sooner had the veteran astronaut been assigned to the mission than he had begun thinking of himself as the presumptive—if not actually crowned—first man on the moon. Now it looked as if all that might be changing, and Aldrin was more than mildly angry. The disgruntled pilot spent considerable time lobbying NASA's senior administrators, insisting that the traditional mission profile be honored and that he be dispatched down the ladder first. Even Aldrin's father, a career military man with a formidable reputation in defense circles, weighed in, working his Pentagon and NASA connections and rallying supporters to his son's cause.

For months leading up to Apollo 11, the question of who would descend the ladder first remained open, until finally, only a short time before launch, a simple, overlooked fact of lunar module design settled the issue: the door of the ship opened inward and to the right. As in all multiman spacecraft, the cockpit of the LEM was laid out so that the commander worked the left side of the instrument panel and his copilot worked the right. In a ship like the lunar module, this apportionment of space was especially important since the cockpit was so small—*barely the size of two phone booths*—that the placement of every switch, throttle, and storage bay had to be planned down to the fraction of an inch. Cramped as the ship was when the astronauts were floating about in it in shirtsleeves, it was even more so when they were dressed in the balloonlike suits and laboring under the suitcaselike backpacks they would have to wear on the lunar surface.

In order to leave this tiny ship, the astronauts would have to open the hatch in the forward portion of the bulkhead and then, one at a time, get down on their hands and knees and back out onto the porchlike platform that led to the descent ladder. The problem was, the latch for the door was on the commander's left-hand side of the ship, which meant the hinges were on the right. As soon as the door was opened and swung inward, the junior pilot would thus be backed against the right wall of the cockpit until the commander had maneuvered his entire body out of the ship and shut the hatch behind him. At that point, the copilot could waddle to the left, open the hatch back up, and follow his commander down.

When this feature of the Apollo 11 lunar module was brought to the attention of Buzz, his father, and his growing group of supporters, even the most ardent Aldrin partisans had to concede defeat. There was a bit of grumbling about allowing the astronauts to swap cockpit positions while they dressed so that Armstrong would be the one flattened against the wall while

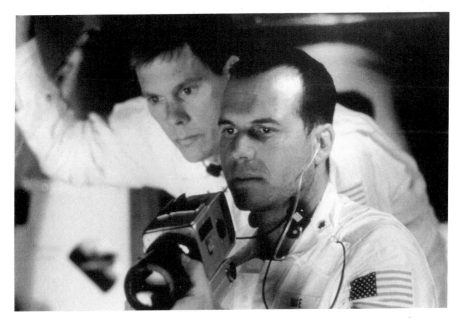

Kevin Bacon and Bill Paxton during pericynthion, the closest approach to the moon.

The lunar module. *(NASA)*

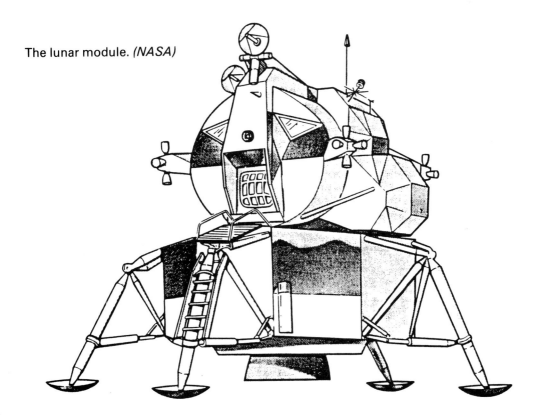

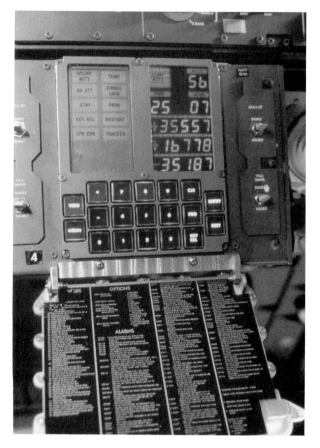

The movie lunar-module computer.

Aldrin egressed, but with space suits and other personal equipment already stowed on the appropriate sides of the ship, even Buzz knew he was licked.

With Armstrong formally preordained the first man on the moon, his rhetorical suitability for the job only now began to be discussed. For months before the mission, NASA was flooded with mail from around the world offering suggestions for the commander's first words on the surface, and public affairs officers within the Agency offered their assistance, making themselves available to sit down with Armstrong and help him cobble together something appropriate to the occasion. Armstrong, however, resisted all such overtures, insisting he could come up with something perfectly adequate—thank you very much—on his own. Whether he ultimately did was open to question.

Though it wasn't politic to say it—and you *wouldn't* say so even if you were asked—you were never completely satisfied with what Neil ultimately

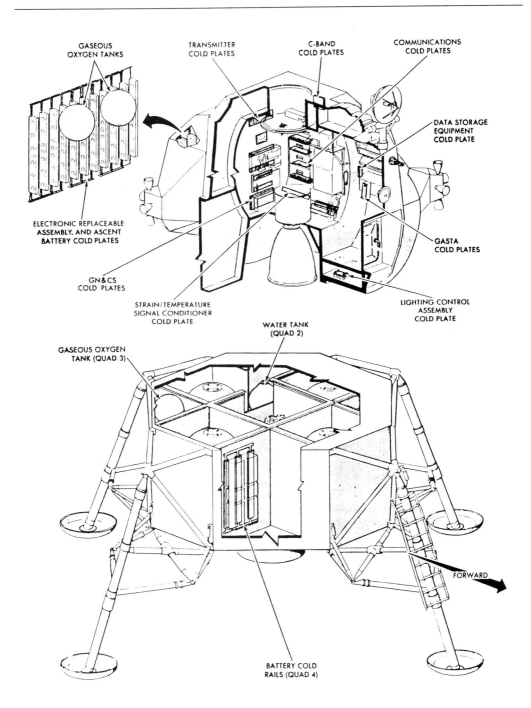

GASEOUS
OXYGEN TANKS

TRANSMITTER
COLD PLATES

C-BAND
COLD PLATES

COMMUNICATIONS
COLD PLATES

DATA STORAGE
EQUIPMENT
COLD PLATE

ELECTRONIC REPLACEABLE
ASSEMBLY, AND ASCENT
BATTERY COLD PLATES

GASTA
COLD PLATES

GN&CS
COLD PLATES

STRAIN/TEMPERATURE
SIGNAL CONDITIONER
COLD PLATE

LIGHTING CONTROL
ASSEMBLY
COLD PLATE

WATER TANK
(QUAD 2)

GASEOUS OXYGEN
TANK (QUAD 3)

FORWARD

BATTERY COLD
RAILS (QUAD 4)

Lunar module temperature control systems. *(NASA)*

The lunar-module (LEM) simulator on the mock-up lunar surface.

settled on, and you believed in your most secret heart that had you been assigned to the flight he was assigned to, you would almost certainly have chosen something better. The biggest problem, of course, was that Neil blew the call. What Armstrong said—and you listened to the tape about a thousand times—was, "That's one small step for man, one giant leap for mankind." That, of course, made no sense. *Man* and *mankind* are interchangeable, and something that's a small step for one is going to be an equally small step for the other. What Neil wanted to say—and what NASA repeatedly insisted that he did say—was, "That's one small step for *a* man, one giant leap for mankind." That, of course, made far more sense, and though Agency spokesmen insisted that the *a* was there and was merely lost in trans-Earth static, nobody believed that was true.

Even if Neil had gotten it right, however, the whole thing still struck you as disappointing. It was too stilted, too planned, too much like the motto on some state or city crest. Ironically, Buzz did a lot better. Relieved of the burden of history and free to say what he was moved to say, he looked around and simply, poetically described what he saw.

"Beautiful, beautiful," the second man on the moon said dreamily, "magnificent desolation."

Though Aldrin's exquisite oxymoron was all but lost to history, you always admired it, and as other men followed Apollo 11 up to the moon and took their first steps on its surface, you were moved and even amused by the words they chose to speak. Apollo 12 commander Pete Conrad, as the shortest man in the astronaut corps, had continually been ribbed about the several-foot leap he would have to make from the bottom of the LEM's descent ladder to its dishlike footpad depressed in the lunar soil. When the time came to make that jump, he decided to join in the joking himself. "Whoopie!" the third man on the moon sang out. "That may have been a small one for Neil, but it's a long one for me."

Three missions later, on Apollo 15, in 1971, Dave Scott took a few moments on the surface to reflect—with genuine eloquence—on humanity's essential and inexplicable need to explore. One mission before that, Al Shepard climbed down the LEM ladder and at first said nothing at all until his capcom, watching on TV, prompted him.

"Okay, Al," the voice from Houston called up. "It looks like you're about on the bottom step. On the surface."

Shepard let a moment play out as if to process that that was indeed true, then offered a response that was nothing if not understated:

"You're right. Al is on the surface."

Of course, it wasn't just on the lunar surface that your fellow pilots made their most memorable observations. At almost every moment in a mission to the moon, there could be some milestone, some critical maneuver that brought you steadily, dramatically closer to the lunar touchdown you had come up here for in the first place. There was the moment in your translunar coast when you separated from the Saturn 5's third-stage booster, turned to face it, and watched as its four petal-like panels opened up, revealing the gold foil-

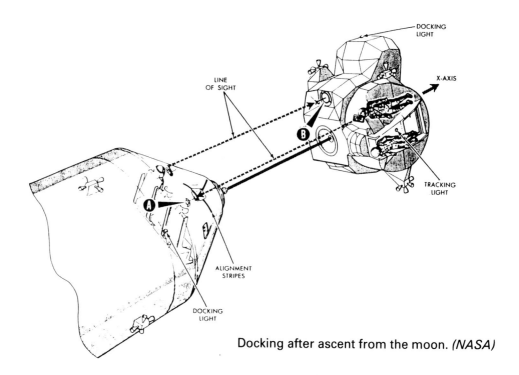

Docking after ascent from the moon. *(NASA)*

covered lunar module nestled inside. There was the slow ballet in which you would inch forward, dock with the lander, and gently extract it from the spent rocket. There was the arrival at the moon, when you would fire your service module engine to drop into lunar orbit. There was the moment—one part heroic, one part poignant, one part scary—when you and one of your fellow pilots would crawl into the LEM through the tunnel that connected the twin ships, while the third member of the team would remain behind. There was then, at last, the descent to the surface, the actual landing, and later, finally, the moonwalk itself.

What you might be motivated to say to your crewmates during any of these remarkable moments you could not imagine. But you knew one thing: whatever you said on the open microphones that transmitted your words to Earth would not be what you would say in utter privacy to the two men alone with you in the ships. The three of you were making this preposterous journey, the three of you understood it best, and only when the air-to-ground loop was switched off and there were just three of you to discuss it would your true thoughts come out. The cockpits of both the command module and the lunar

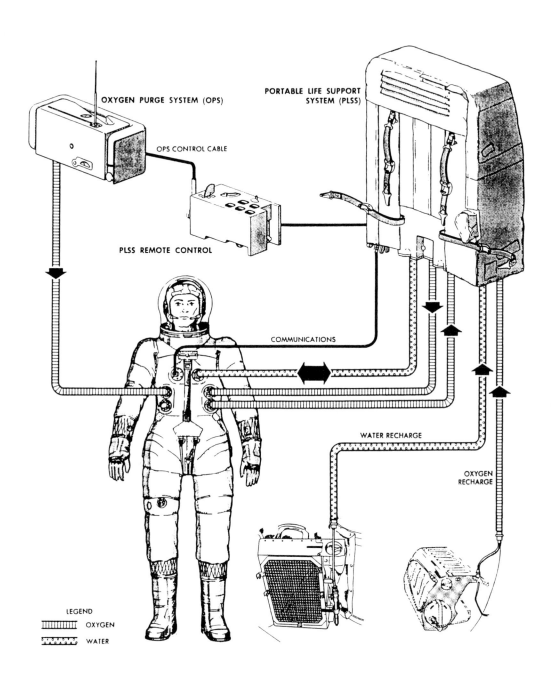

OXYGEN PURGE SYSTEM (OPS)

PORTABLE LIFE SUPPORT
SYSTEM (PLSS)

OPS CONTROL CABLE

PLSS REMOTE CONTROL

COMMUNICATIONS

WATER RECHARGE

OXYGEN
RECHARGE

LEGEND

OXYGEN

WATER

Diagram of the portable life-support system. *(NASA)*

module were equipped with an automatic flight recorder similar to those used in commercial airplanes. Known to NASA engineers as the DSE—for data storage equipment—recordings, the voice records were more colloquially dubbed "dump tapes" for their tendency to pick up whatever was said no matter how unguarded or unedited.

During a mission, dump-tape recordings could be played to Mission Control on a private channel not accessible to the press, and on rare occasions they were—such as when a crew member was sick or a spacecraft system was threatening to fail and the doctors or engineers wanted to dope out the problem before going public with it. More often, however, the recordings weren't played until the crew returned to Earth and the tapes could be removed from the cockpit and transcribed at leisure. When they were, the astronauts' privacy was still respected, and both the recordings and the typed transcripts were kept under the tightest security, treated as classified government material, to be declassified only after twelve years. A mere handful of people would ever listen to the tapes or read the transcripts before that time, but as an astronaut you were among that handful. What you read and heard was illuminating.

CONFIDENTIAL

Apollo 10

Tom Stafford: commander
John Young: command module pilot
Gene Cernan: lunar module pilot

MAY 21, 1969

75 hours, 54 minutes, 22 seconds, mission elapsed time
Arrival at the moon and preparation for engine burn that will drop spacecraft into lunar orbit.
CERNAN: That moon is beautiful! We're right on top of it!
STAFFORD: Oh, shit!
CERNAN: We're right on top of it. I can see it—
STAFFORD: Oh, shit, John. It looks like a big plaster-of-paris cast.
CERNAN: That's incredible.
STAFFORD: It looks like we're close.

CERNAN: That's incredible.

STAFFORD: It does look like we're—well, we're about sixty miles, I guess.

CERNAN: It does look—look gray, doesn't it.

STAFFORD: Shit, baby, we have arrived! It's a big gray plaster-of-paris thing.

CERNAN: That's incredible.

STAFFORD: Okay, let's keep going; we've got to watch this bear here.

YOUNG: Put your head back in the cockpit, Gene-o.

---

76 hours, 3 minutes, 24 seconds, mission elapsed time

Completion of engine burn; spacecraft now in lunar orbit.

STAFFORD: Oh, man! Oh, man! Look at those shallow craters!

CERNAN: I guess we has arrived.

STAFFORD: You better believe it.

YOUNG: I'll tell you something, they *are* craters!

STAFFORD: Get some pictures, you guys.

YOUNG: That's the weirdest-looking surface. There's some color in that.

STAFFORD: It's a brownish gray, old buddy.

CERNAN: Like a big sandbox, though, isn't it?

STAFFORD: Yes.

CERNAN: We is at the moon, fellows! Can you believe that?

STAFFORD: Yes, I can believe it.

CERNAN: Well, what do we do now? *(Laughter)* Read the flight plan, I guess.

---

77 hours, 48 minutes, 21 seconds, mission elapsed time

The spacecraft passes into lunar shadow. Below, the moon's surface vanishes into blackness; above, stars appear.

YOUNG: I don't think I'm going to get any sleep tonight. You know, if this rendezvous and all that stuff works like it's supposed to, this is going to be one hell of a lot of fun. If it don't, shit.

CERNAN: Hey, let me ask you a question. Where do you suppose a planet like this comes from? Do you suppose it broke away from the—away from the Earth like a lot of people say?

YOUNG: Don't ask me, babe.

CERNAN: It sure looks different.

YOUNG: I ain't no cosmologist. I don't care nothing about that.

CERNAN: Sure looks different.

STAFFORD: I just know we're here and it's tremendous to be here.

CERNAN: Yes, but think where it all got started.

YOUNG: Just think of where we're all going though, one of these days. This is just the beginning. There must be some real smart folks out there. They sure keep a bunch of stars out there for them. You realize this is the first dark we've been in since we left that damn planet. First time I ever felt warm about the dark.

Apollo 15

Dave Scott: commander

Al Worden: command module pilot

Jim Irwin: lunar module pilot

JULY 29, 1971

84 hours, 24 minutes, 57 seconds, mission elapsed time

The crew eats dinner in lunar orbit and prepares to go to bed for the night. The next morning, Scott and Irwin will attempt their landing on the moon.

WORDEN: Ah, let's see; yes, we're ready to go over here; 84:24, at about 84:33 we better do all that business. In the meantime, grab a bite. What are we having?

SCOTT: Pork and scalloped potatoes.

IRWIN: It's not bad.

SCOTT: You know, I don't know why it is; every night at this time my nose gets stuffy.

IRWIN: Mine does, too.

SCOTT: Hey, Jim. You know what I do tomorrow?

IRWIN: Can't guess.

SCOTT: Let's go shoot a landing. I'm ready. I'm ready to put that baby right in there, right now.

WORDEN: Yes, sir. You better.

IRWIN: I think the first thing I'm going to do when we get back?

SCOTT: What's that?

IRWIN: Have a beautiful night in Tahiti.

WORDEN: Hey, you're on, buddy. You're on, you're on!

IRWIN: No, really. You ought to really think about it.

SCOTT: Me, too. Big airliner.

IRWIN: Without the aviation.

Apollo 12

Pete Conrad: commander

Dick Gordon: command module pilot

Al Bean: lunar module pilot

NOVEMBER 18, 1969

101 hours, 29 minutes, 00 seconds, mission elapsed time

The morning of the lunar landing. The veteran Conrad and the rookie Bean prepare to move into the lunar module and descend to the surface; Gordon will remain behind in the command module.

BEAN: I'm about as jumpy as I can be this morning!

CONRAD: You noticed!

BEAN: Huh? Jumpier than I was on launch day.

CONRAD: I kind of have the same feeling. It's a bigger day.

BEAN: It is. You've got more things under your command today. Launch day, you're just kind of along for the ride. Be safe, stick with that list. Stick to the list and be careful you don't throw the wrong switch. Don't get in a hurry. Don't get too fancy.

CONRAD: No fancy shit; you're right.

BEAN: Damn! Do I have a lot of breakfast here. See how my pulse is doing. It's a minute above normal.

CONRAD: What's normal?

BEAN: Seventeen in a fifteen-second period. That's what I've been running; I've been checking myself. I used to multiply it out and then I said to hell with it. . . . It'll be good to get down on the lunar surface and do some physical work, you know that?

CONRAD: Speak for yourself; I'm a lazy son of a bitch.

BEAN: So am I. I'm just ready to get down there. . . . If we pull this off, we'll be slicker than owlshit.

CONRAD: It's driving me buggy; I just don't know what I'm going to see when I pitch [the LEM] over [during descent]. Take a look and I'm going to say, "Ahhhhh! There it is!" [Or] I'm going to say, "I don't recognize nothing!" Then I'm in deep yogurt.

BEAN: If you don't recognize a thing, I'll look—just tell me and I'll look out my side.

CONRAD: *(Pointing out window)* That's that—that's that crater vent tube.

BEAN: How'd we ever get here anyway? Why would a guy want to put his ass on the line like this?

---

109 hours, 29 minutes, 26 seconds, mission elapsed time

Conrad and Bean are alone in the LEM as Conrad pilots the ship down to the lunar surface. One of the astronauts' tasks upon landing will be to salvage parts from the unmanned Surveyor probe, which touched down on the moon in 1967.

CONRAD: Man, there's a lunar surface!

BEAN: We're going down, Pete babe.

CONRAD: Yes, I know.

BEAN: Fly that thing in there.

CONRAD: I'll do my best.

BEAN: I know it.

CONRAD: I just hope it's enough.

BEAN: *(Looking out window)* That's so beautiful, Pete. Look there.

CONRAD: I can't look. I ain't going to look out.

BEAN: Okay, if you can't look out, I ain't going to look out. *(Pause)* Nothing for me to do right now. Not a thing for me to do, Pete. *(Pause)* You locked on with the rendezvous radar?

CONRAD: No, why?

BEAN: I didn't know if—because you will be down in here for this perilune. I don't think it's—

CONRAD: I didn't need it for the other.

BEAN: I know it, I know it. I just didn't know if you were yet. What a machine! What a machine! *(Looking out window)* If we take this picture, it'll be famous forever. Even better than when we grab the Surveyor by all of its parts, dismantling it handily.

CONRAD: Boy, this thing sure flies nice.

BEAN: Just like you landed anytime on Earth, Pete.

CONRAD: Okay.

BEAN: I'm not kidding.

CONRAD: What?

BEAN: The closer I get, the more I feel like it's just like landing on Earth. Just let it fly down and park it somewhere. We'll bound out and grab a rock.

CONRAD: Okay.

---

110 hours, 3 minutes, 13 seconds, mission elapsed time

Conrad and Bean make their final approach and land.

CONRAD: The hell we aren't getting low.

BEAN: Don't think about it; it's easier.

CONRAD: What's that whistling anyhow? What is that?

BEAN: I don't know. *(Pause)* Hope your pulse is lower than mine.

CONRAD: It's not too bad right at the moment. *(Pause)* Man, there's some mighty big mountains out there. Look at them.

BEAN: I was just thinking about that a while ago. We'll shoot right between a couple of them.

CONRAD: Man, oh, man, we're getting low. Ho, ho, ho.

BEAN: That's right. You can't land if you don't get down there amongst them.

CONRAD: Standing by for throttle up, Houston.

BEAN: Pete, it looks good.

CONRAD: Throttle up.

BEAN: It really feels good when it comes up. Feels good to be standing in the g field again. Okay, two minutes and thirty seconds, 44,700 [feet in altitude], looks good.

CONRAD: About forty-four feet per second fast, about six feet per second low on H-dot, and about one hundred feet low on altitude. Looking good.

BEAN: Looking good, looking good. AGS are hanging right in there. Supercrit hangs at eleven hundred or twelve—all the time.

CONRAD: Okay, we're out at thirty-five thousand.

BEAN: PNGS and AGS agree. Fantastic! Let's give it another update.

CONRAD: Throttle down!

BEAN: Throttle down!

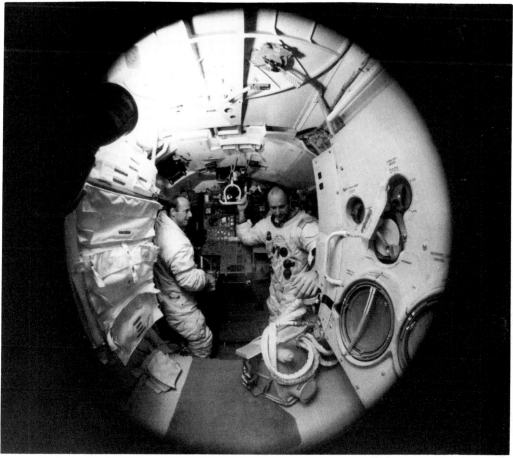

A fish-eye lens view of Apollo 12 astronauts Charles Conrad, Jr., commander, and Alan Bean, lunar module pilot, inside the lunar-module simulator in October 1969. *(NASA)*

CONRAD: One hundred sixty feet a second, huh?

BEAN: We'll be there in a minute.

CONRAD: Passing twelve thousand feet. Spring-loaded to go grab that Surveyor. I'm trying to cheat and look out there; I think I see my crater.

BEAN: Pitching over.

CONRAD: Hey, there it is! There it is! Son of a gun! Right down the middle of the road!

BEAN: Outstanding. Forty-two degrees, Pete.

CONRAD: That's so fantastic, I can't believe it.

BEAN: We're at two thousand feet.

CONRAD: How far?

BEAN: The boys on the ground do okay. Eighteen hundred feet up, thirty-nine degrees.

CONRAD: Okay.

BEAN: One thousand feet, coming down at thirty; you're looking good. Got fourteen percent fuel. Looks good out there, babe. Looks good. Thirty-two degrees; you're at eight hundred feet. Thirty-three degrees, at six hundred eighty feet. Thirty-three degrees, six hundred feet. Antenna's okay.

CONRAD: Right.

BEAN: Thirty-five degrees. You're at five hundred thirty feet, Pete. Five hundred thirty. You're all right!

CONRAD: I got it.

BEAN: Eleven percent [of fuel remaining]. Loads of gas. Three hundred feet, coming down at five [feet per second].

CONRAD: Hey, look at that crater! Right where it's supposed to be! Hey, you're beautiful.

BEAN: Ten percent. Two hundred feet. Coming down at three [feet per second]. Need to come down.

CONRAD: Okay.

BEAN: One hundred ninety feet. Come on down. One hundred eighty feet. Nine percent. You're looking good. We'll get some dust before long. One hundred thirty feet. One hundred twenty-four feet, Pete. One hundred twenty feet, coming down at six. You got nine percent, eight percent. You're looking okay. Ninety-six feet, coming down at six. Slow down the descent rate.

CONRAD: Forty-two feet, coming down at six.

BEAN: Coming down at two. Start the clock. Forty-two feet, coming down at two. Looking good; watch the dust. Thirty-one, thirty-two, thirty feet. Coming down at two, Pete. You've got plenty of gas, plenty of gas, babe. Stay in there. Eighteen feet, coming in at two. You've got it made. Come on in there. *(Six seconds later)* Contact light!

CONRAD: Okay.

BEAN: Good landing, Pete! Outstanding, man!

CONRAD: Master arm, on.

BEAN: Beautiful!

CONRAD: Descent vent, fire.

BEAN: It's beautiful out there!

CONRAD: It sure is. It's something else.

Kevin Bacon and Tom Hanks in the command module during the accident.

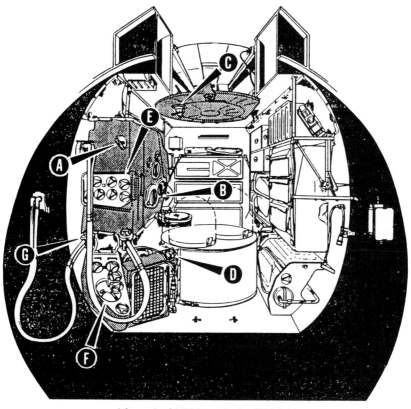

Aft end of LEM cockpit. *(NASA)*

Apollo 14

Alan Shepard: commander
Stu Roosa: command module pilot
Ed Mitchell: lunar module pilot

FEBRUARY 4, 1971

113 hours, 19 minutes, 39 seconds, mission elapsed time
Shepard and Mitchell help one another don their suits and prepare to take their first walk on the lunar surface.
MITCHELL: Okay, PLSS fan on. Right vent flag—right vent flag, cleared.
SHEPARD: Right vent flag is cleared. Tone is stopped.
MITCHELL: Okay, my tone is stopped. Okay, don helmets.
SHEPARD: Okay. Is your drink bag positioned okay?
MITCHELL: I think I got a mouth full of microphone; I can't get a drink.
SHEPARD: You've got to put up with a few hardships.
MITCHELL: Right, I don't mind at all.
SHEPARD: Okay, you're ready to go out and play in the snow.
MITCHELL: Yes, it looks like my snowsuit is ready.

Apollo 16

John Young: commander
Ken Mattingly: command module pilot
Charlie Duke: lunar module pilot

APRIL 21, 1972

129 hours, 49 minutes, 00 seconds, mission elapsed time
Young and Duke walk on the surface of the moon. At the insistence of the flight surgeon, the astronauts have been drinking potassium-spiked orange juice in order to replenish their electrolytes.
YOUNG: I got the farts again. I got 'em again, Charlie. I don't know what the hell gives them to me. I think it's the acid in the stomach.
DUKE: It probably is.
YOUNG: I mean, I haven't eaten this much citrus fruit in twenty years. And I'll tell you one thing: in another twelve fucking days, I ain't never eating any more. And if they offer to serve me potassium with my breakfast, I'm going to throw up. I like an occasional orange, I really do. But I'll be damned if I'm going to be buried in oranges.

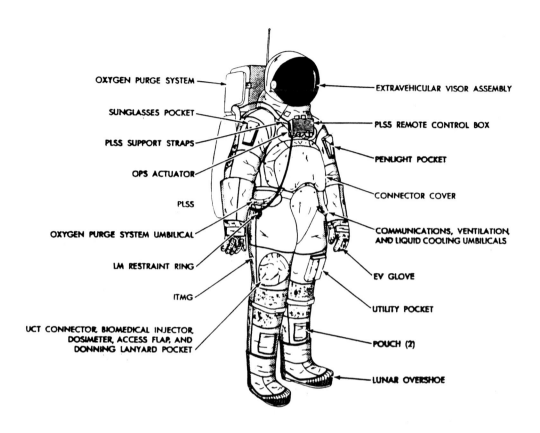

OXYGEN PURGE SYSTEM

SUNGLASSES POCKET

PLSS SUPPORT STRAPS

OPS ACTUATOR

PLSS

OXYGEN PURGE SYSTEM UMBILICAL

LM RESTRAINT RING

ITMG

UCT CONNECTOR, BIOMEDICAL INJECTOR, DOSIMETER, ACCESS FLAP, AND DONNING LANYARD POCKET

EXTRAVEHICULAR VISOR ASSEMBLY

PLSS REMOTE CONTROL BOX

PENLIGHT POCKET

CONNECTOR COVER

COMMUNICATIONS, VENTILATION, AND LIQUID COOLING UMBILICALS

EV GLOVE

UTILITY POCKET

POUCH (2)

LUNAR OVERSHOE

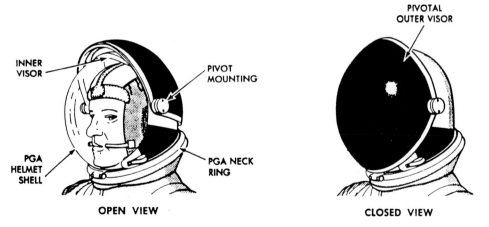

INNER VISOR

PIVOT MOUNTING

PGA HELMET SHELL

PGA NECK RING

OPEN VIEW

PIVOTAL OUTER VISOR

CLOSED VIEW

A lunar space suit. *(NASA)*

CAPCOM: Orion, Houston.

YOUNG: Yes, sir.

CAPCOM: You have a hot mike.

YOUNG: How long have we had that?

CAPCOM: It's been on throughout the debriefing.

YOUNG: Sorry about that. It's terrible being on a hot mike sometimes.

Apollo 10

Tom Stafford: commander

John Young: command module pilot

Gene Cernan: lunar module pilot

MAY 23, 1969

137 hours, 40 minutes, 42 seconds, mission elapsed time

On the far side of the moon, out of contact with Houston, the astronauts have completed the engine burn that will bring them back to Earth.

CERNAN: Oh, babe. Good show. Now we're on our way home.

YOUNG: What do we—what do we do now?

CERNAN: What?

YOUNG: What does it say to do now?

CERNAN: I'm going to get out my music!

STAFFORD: I think the best words to start with [when radio contact is reacquired] are, "Houston, we're on our way back to Earth."

CERNAN: Man. We're coming home.

NATIONAL AERONAUTICS AND SPACE ADMINISTRATION
NEWS

Release No. 70–76
For immediate release: May 22, 1970

A National Aeronautics and Space Administration scientist reported today that a microorganism, thought to have been accidentally deposited on the Surveyor III camera prior to its launch to the moon three years ago, was recovered from inside the camera when it was returned to Earth by the Apollo 12 crew in November 1969.

Frederick J. Mitchell, a microbiologist in NASA's Lunar Receiving Laboratory at the Manned Spacecraft Center, Houston, said the microorganism—*Streptococcus miti*—apparently survived the launch, the three-day Moon-bound journey in the vacuum of space, and 950 days in the hostile lunar environment. The organism was found after extensive laboratory testing of the camera parts in Houston.

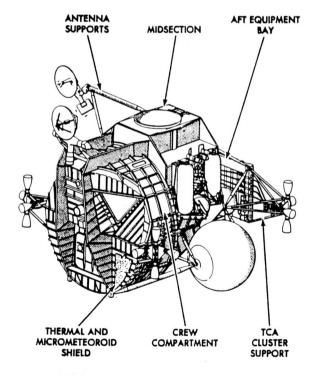

LEM ascent stage structure. *(NASA)*

NATIONAL AERONAUTICS AND SPACE ADMINISTRATION
NEWS

Message from the Premier of the Cook Islands following splashdown of Apollo 12

On this historic occasion in space exploration and the splashdown of Apollo 12 in Cook Islands' waters and the second splashdown of an Apollo flight in our small territory, the Premier and the people of the Cook Islands offer their warmest greetings and congratulations.

Sincerely,
A. R. Henry

Moscow: TASS International Service in English; 15:00 GMT; 31 Jul. 71

ASTRONAUTS LEAVE LUNAR MODULE

New York—At 01 hours and 16 minutes Moscow time today, the lunar module of the spacecraft "Apollo-15" with astronauts D. Scott and J. Irwin on board landed in the area of the lunar Apennines. The third astronaut, A. Worden, remained in the ship's command module in lunar orbit. After a rest the astronauts prepared to go out onto the lunar surface. The first to leave the module was the ship's commander, D. Scott. He was followed by J. Irwin a few minutes later.

Moscow: TASS International Service in English; 24 Jul. 71

NEW BOOK SHOWS CUBA'S DEPENDENCE ON SOCIALIST CAMP

Dushanbe, Tadzhikistana—Year after year, Soviet people's interest in the fiery island of freedom grows. Quite recently, a book devoted to the problems of Cuba's foreign economic relations was fast disappearing from the counters of the Dushanbe "Nauka" bookshop. The book is devoted to the turnabout effected in foreign economic relations and stresses that this turnabout only became possible because of the existence of the world socialist system.

Moscow: TASS International Service in English; 13:45 GMT; 8 Aug. 71

PODGORNY CONGRATULATES NIXON ON SUCCESS OF APOLLO-15

Moscow—The President of the Presidium of the USSR Supreme Soviet, Nikolay Podgorny has congratulated the United States President, Richard Nixon, on the successful completion of the "Apollo-15" spaceship flight to the moon. He asked to convey congratulations and good wishes to courageous cosmonauts David Scott, Alfred Worden, and James Irwin.

Washington Post; Aug. 3, 1971 (Reuter)

APOLLO 15 BORES FRENCH CRITIC

Paris—A lone dissenting voice in the French news industry today described the live television picture of the Apollo 15 moon mission as "an unspeakable bore." In his weekly column in the mass circulation *France Soir,* novelist and TV critic Jean Dutourd said

Tom Hanks and Bill Paxton rehearsing the Apollo 13 moonwalk that was never to be.

Apollo was one of the things that made him walk away from his set. "It must be confessed that these experiments are an unspeakable bore," he wrote.

Yugoslavian News Service; 26 Jan. 72

U.S. ASTRONAUTS

Zagreb—Vice President of the Assembly of Croatia, Boris Bakrac, this morning received American Astronauts David Scott, Alfred Worden, and James Irwin, who are on a two-day visit to Zagreb. Also this morning, the three members of the Apollo-15 crew met with President of the Yugoslav Academy of Sciences and Arts Dr. Grga Novak and other academicians.

Yugoslavian News Service in Serbo-Croatian; 1 Feb. 72

PRISON SENTENCES FOR CROATIANS

Zagreb—Petar Zulicek, 33, from Sestranec, an employee of the post-telegraph-telephone office in Zagreb, was found guilty by the Varazdin District Court Council of ridiculing the Socialist Federal Republic of Yugoslavia and its highest representatives in the presence of several witnesses at a bowling alley. For this as well as inciting national intolerance, Petar Zulicek was sentenced to a 6-month prison term.

New York Times; April 22, 1972

MONTANANS SEND NIXON ROCKS AS MOON PROTEST

Helena, Mont.—An activist group sent President Nixon a box of rocks to protest the Apollo 16 moon mission. The Montana State Low Income Organization said the purpose of the costly moon program appeared to be merely the collection of rocks. The Montana rocks, the spokesman said, are free.

NATIONAL AERONAUTICS AND SPACE ADMINISTRATION
Washington, D.C.

May 26, 1972

Mr. Edward A. Taylor
Executive Director
Florida Citrus Commission
State of Florida
Department of Citrus
Lakeland, FL

Dear Mr. Taylor:

Thank you for your thoughtful letter of May 4.

I am indeed aware of the incident concerning the orange drink on the Apollo 16 mission. It is true that astronauts Young and Duke did not realize they had a live mike during one of their exchanges concerning the effects of the orange drink. You can be sure that the crews generally are aware when they are talking to each other privately or whether they are on the air-to-ground loop. Every now and then, they do fail to make sure that the mike is not live and we on the ground hear what they are saying. NASA policy is, and will continue to be, to release all the air-to-ground conversations live to the news media. We feel very strongly about this.

Sincerely,

James C. Fletcher
Administrator

At Hickam Air Force Base in Hawaii on April 18, 1970, President Richard Nixon presents the Presidential Medal of Freedom, the nation's highest civilian award, to the Apollo 13 crew. From left, John Swigert, Fred Haise, Jim Lovell, and Nixon. *(NASA)*

WESTERN UNION

WHA008 (0814) 12 DEC 72, BALTO., MD.

PRESIDENT RICHARD NIXON
WHITE HOUSE
DC

MR. PRESIDENT,

WHEN NEIL AND BUZZ WERE ON THE MOON YOU SPOKE TO THEM. WHEN GENE AND JACK WERE FINISHED ON THE MOON YOU DIDN'T SPEAK TO THEM, WHY?

JIM KIRBY, PRESS DIRECTOR
COMMITTEE TO REELECT THE PRESIDENT, 1972
BALTIMORE COUNTY

GENERAL DECLARATION

(Outward/Inward)

AGRICULTURE, CUSTOMS, IMMIGRATION, AND PUBLIC HEALTH

Owner or Operator .... NATIONAL AERONAUTICS AND SPACE ADMINISTRATION ....

Marks of
Nationality and Registration ..... U.S.A. ..... Flight No. APOLLO 11 ..... Date ..... JULY 24, 1969

Departure from .... MOON .... Arrival at ..... HONOLULU, HAWAII, U.S.A.
(Place and Country) ..... (Place and Country)

FLIGHT ROUTING

("Place" Column always to list origin, every en-route stop and destination)

PLACE	TOTAL NUMBER OF CREW	NUMBER OF PASSENGERS ON THIS STAGE	CARGO
CAPE KENNEDY	COMMANDER NEIL A. ARMSTRONG		
MOON	*Neil A. Armstrong* (signature)	Departure Place:	MOON ROCK AND MOON DUST SAMPLES Cargo Manifests Attached
JULY 24, 1969 HONOLULU	COLONEL EDWIN E. ALDRIN, JR.	Embarking NIL Through on same flight NIL	
	Edwin E. Aldrin Jr. (signature)	Arrival Place:	
	M. Collins (signature)	Disembarking NIL Through on same flight NIL	
	LT. COLONEL MICHAEL COLLINS		

Declaration of Health

Persons on board known to be suffering from illness other than airsickness or the effects of accidents, as well as those cases of illness disembarked during the flight:

NONE

Any other condition on board which may lead to the spread of disease:

TO BE DETERMINED

Details of each disinsecting or sanitary treatment (place, date, time, method) during the flight. If no disinsecting has been carried out during the flight give details of most recent disinsecting:

Signed, if required ....
Crew Member Concerned

For official use only

HONOLULU AIRPORT

Honolulu, Hawaii

ENTERED

Ernest I. Murai (signature)
Customs Inspector

I declare that all statements and particulars contained in this General Declaration, and in any supplementary forms required to be presented with this General Declaration are complete, exact and true to the best of my knowledge and that all through passengers will continue/have continued on the flight.

NATIONAL AERONAUTICS AND SPACE ADMINISTRATION
Washington, D.C.

Nov. 10, 1972

Mr. David Gergen
Staff Assistant
The White House
Washington, D.C. 20500

SUBJECT: Apollo 17 Commemorative Plaque

Dear Dave:

Attached for White House Approval is NASA's suggested commemorative plaque to be left on the moon on Apollo 17 attached to the lunar module as on Apollo 11.

The Apollo 11 plaque inscription was:

HERE MEN FROM THE PLANET EARTH

FIRST SET FOOT UPON THE MOON

JULY 1969, A.D.

WE CAME IN PEACE FOR ALL MANKIND

Dr. Fletcher's proposed inscription for the Apollo 17 plaque is:

HERE MEN FROM THE PLANET EARTH

COMPLETED THEIR FIRST VISITS TO THE MOON

DECEMBER 1972, A.D.

WE WILL COME AGAIN IN PEACE FOR ALL MANKIND

For Apollo 17, as on Apollo 11, the plaque would carry the signature of the three astronauts and the President, assuming the president concurs. We still have the President's signature from the Apollo 11 plaque which can be used to inscribe the plaque for Apollo 17.

Sincerely,

George P. Chandler
Assistant Executive
Secretary

NATIONAL AERONAUTICS AND SPACE ADMINISTRATION
Washington, D.C.

Feb. 7, 1973

Honorable William D. Hathaway
United States Senate
Washington, D.C. 20510

Dear Senator Hathaway,

This is in response to your letter on behalf of your constituent in West Kennebunk, Maine, concerning the cost of our American flags left on the moon by the Apollo astronauts. You will be pleased to know that the flags were standard three and a half foot by five foot nylon flags, provided through the General Services Administration to NASA at a cost of $5.63 each.

Sincerely,

H. Dale Grubb
Assistant Administrator
for Legislative Affairs

San Francisco Examiner, Saturday, April 15, 1972
ARE YOU READY FOR YOUR FIRST RIDE INTO SPACE?
It Could Happen by 1979

Women and nonastronauts such as reporters and artists may go into space as early as 1979, according to Dale D. Meyers, head of NASA's manned spaceflight program. Wernher von Braun, world's foremost rocket designer, predicts that "before the year 2000 is over the first child could be born on the moon."

The predictions came in the wake of President Nixon's January 5 announcement that, Congress willing, the U.S. would commit itself to a revolutionary new space transportation system. Called the space shuttle, this airliner-type craft would take off like a rocket, allow ordinary untrained men or women to spend a week in space, then land them at an airport no more exotic than Los Angeles International.

10

Cooling Down

Actor Wayne Duvall was not dressed for a day on the *Apollo 13* set. He *thought* he was; indeed, he had spent a lot of time picking just the right thing to wear today. But when he arrived, he found he'd fallen short.

It wasn't as if Duvall was accustomed to choosing his outfits when he presented himself on the Universal Studios stages where *Apollo 13* was being filmed. Portraying one of the flight controllers who worked in Mission Control during 1970's near-disastrous lunar mission, he had spent most of his recent work-days in the NASA men's standard-issue uniform of short-sleeve, pastel-colored business shirt, with a tab collar that had long since collapsed from repeated washings, and a narrow black tie just this side of a bolo. The picture was not a pretty one, but it was an accurate one, and throughout Universal's mock-up MOCR, more than two dozen other actors had also spent a significant part of their summer in this kind of unlovely ensemble.

But it was not summer anymore, and the five weeks of filming in Mission Control had recently come to an end. On Universal's

Bill Paxton in the LEM.

Stage 27, the magnificent MOCR (Mission Operations Control Room) replica had already been dismantled—a scuffed tape outline on the cement floor the only evidence that it had existed at all—and the *Apollo 13* crew had now moved a few hundred yards away to Stage 34, where filming would begin on a far smaller but no less remarkable set: the mock-up of the Apollo 13 lunar module named *Aquarius*. It was in the real *Aquarius* that astronauts Jim Lovell, Jack Swigert, and Fred Haise had labored to bring their blast-damaged Apollo 13 spacecraft back to Earth, and it was in this replica of that ship that Tom Hanks, Kevin Bacon, and Bill Paxton would work to bring the astronauts' experiences to film.

Visiting the new set on a warm October day, Duvall was happy to be dressed fashionably for once, wearing casual summer slacks and a light sport jacket. As he reached the door, however, a production assistant stopped him.

"You're not going in there wearing that, are you?" she asked.

"Why? I'm overdressed?"

"Underdressed. *Way* underdressed."

Duvall stood confusedly for a moment while a coat, hat, gloves, and scarf were fetched from the wardrobe trailer and thrown hurriedly about him. Only when the production assistant was satisfied that he was properly swaddled did she open the door of the stage and beckon him in.

Immediately, Duvall saw that the extra clothing was a good idea. Stage 34, where dozens of crew members, three actors, and one director were grinding out their day's filming, was about as cold as the inside of a refrigerator. Indeed, according to the large, round, clocklike thermometer he spotted on the north wall of the stage, it was actually *colder* than a refrigerator—about thirty-four degrees. Clouds of vapor formed as he exhaled—as they did from a knot of parka-clad people who stood nearby, sipping hot coffee and quietly talking. Off to the side, on the wall by the front door, a safety poster suggested that it might not be such a good idea for any of them to be here at all.

"WARNING!" the sign read. "Know the symptoms of frostbite! Wear gloves, hat, and layers to avoid hypothermia!"

Duvall looked about and laughed in something less than surprise. This was not, he knew, the kind of thing that was supposed to occur in the gracious business of moviemaking. However, it was, he knew, *exactly* the kind of thing that was involved in making *Apollo 13*.

When it came to the costumes, consoles, sets, and props necessary to tell the story of the Apollo 13 lunar mission, director Ron Howard, producer Brian Grazer, and the wardrobe and art departments decided early on that absolute historical accuracy was a nonnegotiable goal. Instrument panels would not be painted a photogenic robin's-egg blue if the real panels had been a less camera-friendly green. Space suits would not be sewn from lightweight cotton if the genuine articles had been of a bulkier, less flexible canvas. Console switches would not be identified with easy-to-understand labels like THRUSTERS if the real switches in the real ship had been labeled a far more arcane RCS, QUAD A. Most important, the conditions inside both the command module *Odyssey* and the lunar module *Aquarius* would not be made comfortable for the actors who would be portraying Jim Lovell, Jack Swigert, and Fred Haise if they had not been comfortable for Lovell, Swigert, and Haise themselves. For Tom Hanks, Kevin Bacon, and Bill Paxton, this was not necessarily good news.

When Apollo 13 was limping back toward Earth, the absence of all power in its command module and most of the power in its lunar module meant a loss of virtually all environmental systems—including those that generated heat. Losing heat is not a good thing in translunar space, where temperatures can rise as high as 280 degrees Fahrenheit in the unfiltered glare of the sun, but drop as low as 280 below in the shade. Given the tendency of a hot body like a spacecraft to radiate away warmth, the shaded part of space on one side of the ship easily prevailed over the sunny part on the other, and the temperature inside the cockpit quickly plummeted. For the better part of a week, Lovell, Swigert, and Haise survived in their spacecraft at barely thirty-four degrees, with little more than body heat, one-layer beta-cloth jumpsuits, and dreamy visions of a South Pacific splashdown to keep them warm.

For the producers of the *Apollo 13* movie, simulating these iceboxlike conditions at first seemed straightforward. The condensation that formed on all of the ship's metal surfaces could easily be re-created with a misting gun; the thin layer of ice that appeared on its windows could be duplicated with frostlike paint; even the suffering of the three crewmen could be reasonably well simulated by actors who remembered what it felt like to be stuck at a bus stop or on a train platform with too thin a topcoat on too cold a day.

What couldn't be re-created without genuine cold—and without a little genuine suffering—however, was the singular sign of frigid temperatures: visible breath. As soon as Ron Howard began planning Apollo 13's return-to-Earth scenes, he knew that if his audience was going to believe his actors were cold, they were going to have to see them exhale; and for that to happen, the temperature on the set was going to have to fall for real.

Refrigerating a space as large as a movie stage is not an easy matter, and to bring about this literally chilling effect, Howard, Grazer, and their technical crew had to call upon Agrekko, Inc., a company that designs and installs cooling systems for hotels, industries, retail facilities and, increasingly, the entertainment industry. When the *Apollo 13* team contacted Agrekko and explained their needs, the company knew it would have its hands full. Universal's Stage 34 is big, measuring 170,000 cubic feet. Though the lunar-module set where the filming would take place was tiny—smaller than the cockpit of an average airliner—it was impossible to refrigerate that space alone, since at any moment, at least one of the module's walls would be missing, allowing the cameras in, but allowing the cold air out. This meant that the entire stage—wall to distant wall, floor to distant ceiling—would have to be cooled. Making things more complicated, that cooling would have to be precisely done. Before breath could become visible in so huge a space, the average air temperature would have to be lowered to between twenty-eight and thirty-four degrees, and the humidity would have to be raised to an almost rain-producing level. To complicate matters further, Universal's Stage 36 would also have to be refrigerated so that shooting could occur simultaneously on both stages.

The temperature-lowering part of the problem could be handled fairly straightforwardly. Agrekko envisioned installing a 150-ton, van-size water chiller outside Stage 34 and connecting it to a 3,000-watt generator. Inside the chiller would be one hundred gallons of glycol and water mixed together in a 55–45 ratio. What's nice about water, of course, is that it can get extremely cold; what's nice about glycol is that it doesn't easily freeze. Mix the two of them into a single solution and you get a liquid that can be chilled well below the freezing point—as low as seventeen degrees Fahrenheit—without ever turning to ice. When the glycol-water mix was refrigerated to this bitterly cold temperature, it would be pumped through ducts to four 150-ton water handlers in each corner of the soundstage, where it would circulate through a closed loop of pipes. Fans in the water handlers would then draw room-temperature air into the body of the unit where it would swirl around this subfreezing tubing. Though the air would remain in contact with the pipes for only a few seconds, it would quickly surrender much of its heat to the circulating water-glycol, dropping to about 22 degrees. This superchilled air would then be blown back onto the stage, causing the temperature of the room as a whole to begin to fall as well.

The system, while good, was not perfect. Cold air, as anyone knows who's ever returned painfully chapped from a day of skiing, is also generally dry air, and no sooner would the overall temperature of the soundstage begin to drop toward freezing than the overall humidity would begin to drop as well—leaving little of the water needed to allow even the warmest breath to become visible. For that reason, at least eight ten-gallon drums of water would have to be installed in the ceiling of Stage 34 and attached to a misting system. About half an hour before the film crew was ready to shoot, the misters would have to be turned on, the cold air would have to be humidified, and then the actors—now presumably steaming like locomotives—could go to work.

The night before *Apollo 13*'s first day of refrigerated filming was scheduled, the air handlers were hooked up and the chillers rumbled ominously to life. Warned that today was the day it would start getting cold, most of the cast and crew members brought along coats, hats, scarves, and gloves, and by 5 P.M.—when the sixty-eight-degree temperature of the stage had dropped to a much more autumnal fifty-two—the winter wear was broken out and donned. Ed Yoon, a production intern, came prepared with a fur-lined, earflap, snap-under-the-chin hat that, while more than amply warm, was less than fashionable. Yoon, however, was not concerned with making a sartorial statement and snapped his cap comfortably in place.

"Hey, Ed," Tom Hanks called out as Yoon passed, *"extremely* snazzy headwear."

"Kind of makes a statement, doesn't it?"

"Oh, it makes a statement, all right," Hanks chuckled.

"Go ahead, laugh today. But tomorrow when it's thirty-two degrees in here, *you're* gonna be wishing you were *me*, Mr. Movie Star."

With that, Yoon turned and walked easily away, and Hanks erupted into laughter. "I love this guy," he said delightedly. "Six months in the business and he already knows not to be impressed by the star."

The next morning when the cast and crew arrived for work, there was noticeably less merriment on Universal's Stage 34. The Agrekko cooling system had been left on for most of the night, and by 8 A.M., the set thermometer was indeed hovering at just above thirty-two degrees. At the moment, the air was still dry, but with the arrival of the crew, the loud, hissing misting

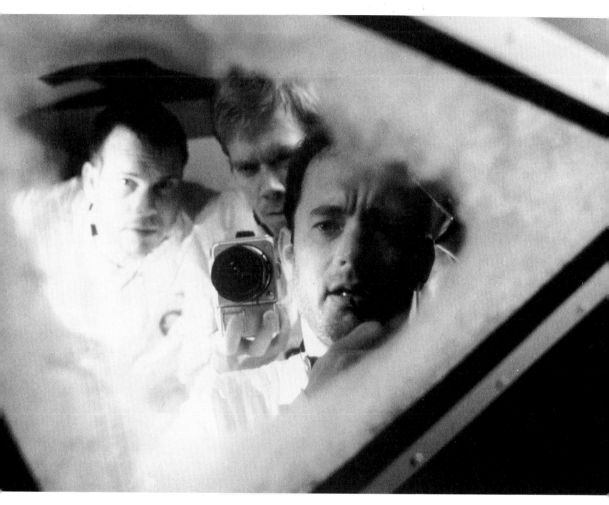

The *Apollo 13* crew staring out the artificially frozen window of the lunar module.

system was turned on as well, and the dry cold on the set was rapidly being transformed into a wet, heavy, humid one.

In the first scene that was scheduled to be filmed in these inhospitable conditions, the Apollo 13 spacecraft is about halfway back to Earth, and the crew—exhausted from three days of cold and stress and lack of rest—at last begins to show signs of fraying nerves. Swigert and Haise would begin snapping at one another over trajectory projections, and Lovell, as skipper, would have to intercede. The material was new, added to the script only in the last few days, and before shooting could begin, Howard wanted a quick run-through to make sure his actors were familiar with it.

"Okay, can we have a rehearsal?" he called to the well-bundled crowd. "Tom, Kevin, Bill?"

Hanks, Bacon, and Paxton immediately appeared from the wings of the stage, dressed, like the rest of the crew, for the winterlike weather. Bacon and Paxton were in heavy quilted coats; Hanks was in a padded maroon wind-breaker decorated with the insignia of Jim Lovell's four space missions. The real Lovell, Swigert, and Haise, of course, had no such cozy outergarments while flying back to Earth aboard the frigid Apollo 13, and so the actors couldn't either. Shucking their coats in the freezing air, the three men hopped into the mock-up lunar module in their white one-piece flight suits alone. Howard called for the noisy misting units to be turned off, and then, at his signal, the actors began their run-through.

"I've been going over the numbers again," Bacon, playing a worried Jack Swigert, began. "We're exceeding escape velocity. They've got us going too damn fast."

"How do you come to that conclusion?" Paxton, as Fred Haise, asked.

"I know how to add," Bacon snapped.

"Half the Ph.D.s on the planet are down there working on this thing," said Hanks placatingly.

"And if they made a mistake and there's no way to reverse it, do you think they'd tell us?" Bacon asked. "There's no reason for them to tell us."

"What do you mean they're not going to tell us?" Paxton asked.

"Look, there's a thousand things we have to do to get back there, Jack," Hanks said. "We're on number eight and you're on about number six hundred ninety-two."

The scene played out for another minute or two with the tension among

Kevin Bacon on Stage 34 in the refrigerated command module.

the three characters growing steadily, until Hanks, as Lovell, put a stop to the quarreling:

"That's it! We are *not* going to do this! We can bounce off the walls for fifteen minutes but we're still going to wind up right here with the same problem: trying to figure out how not to die. So stow it!"

The rehearsal concluded and Howard smiled. The actors had done their homework, and the new material was going to work well. What wasn't working as well, however, was the cold. Even with the air as heavy and wet as it was, there was still not enough visible condensation coming from the astronauts, and before actual filming could begin, things would have to get heavier and wetter still.

"Can we get the misters back on?" Howard said to Aldric Porter, his first assistant director.

"Misters on!" Porter called out to the technicians in the wings.

"Misters on!" someone answered.

With that, a loud, watery hiss once again began in the rafters, and a shroud of thick, visible condensation began to descend on the set.

"Clouding up," someone muttered, looking ceilingward.

"Expect flurries by lunch," someone answered.

Not everybody working on *Apollo 13* today would have to be worrying about snowfall before noon. Just next door, on Stage 36, where the refrigeration system had not yet been turned on, executive producer and second-unit director Todd Hallowell was shooting some additional scenes, and on the set where Hallowell was working, things were a lot balmier. On most movie crews, the second-unit director oversees a sort of mini film crew within the main film crew, working with his own cinematographer, his own cameramen, and his own technical team. The job of the second-unit director is to film some of the screenplay's secondary, supporting scenes, which the director himself could not realistically handle if he had any expectation of completing the movie on time. Though the second-unit director's work does not usually get as much recognition as the director's, it can be pretty impressive stuff. According to the *Apollo 13* filming schedule, Hallowell's second-unit crew would be responsible for the aerial footage of the Kennedy Space Center, the sunrise footage of the Saturn 5 launch site, the helicopter footage above the deck of the recovery ship, and the dramatic press-conference footage in which skeptical reporters interrogate NASA officials about just what is wrong with the Apollo 13 spacecraft and just what has to be done to bring the crew home alive.

Today, Hallowell was filming what were known as inserts—close-up shots of instrument-panel switches and knobs that could be interspersed with the principal footage when the script called for the astronauts to be executing a maneuver of some kind. Insert work is not always terribly dramatic to watch, but with a filming break on Stage 34 while the misters did their work and with the climate on Stage 36 at least thirty degrees warmer and a lot drier, Hallowell found he had an unaccustomed audience this morning.

"You people look *too* comfortable in here," Michael Rosenberg, Imagine Films' senior vice president of marketing, said as he entered Stage 36 with about a dozen other parka-clad people and headed straight for the coffee urn.

Bill Paxton as Fred Haise in the frozen lunar module.

"Don't you think you ought to lower the temperature at least a little bit, if only as a gesture of solidarity?"

"Hey," Hallowell said with a shrug, "I canceled Hawaiian Shirt Day. I think I made a gesture."

Before long, word went out that Stage 34 was down to its desired temperature and up to its desired moisture level, and the crew, only now warming up, trudged reluctantly back over. The actual filming of the argument scene—Scene 220 in a screenplay with a total of 338—began about 10 A.M., continued throughout the remainder of the day, resumed the next day, and was not wrapped up until the day after that. The scene had to be shot from numerous angles; the LEM mock-up had to be moved into numerous positions to accommodate those angles; and since the scene was not being filmed in zero g, numerous pieces of additional equipment had to be used to allow the actors to appear weightless.

Paxton and Hanks would spend much of those three days sitting on bobbing, seesawlike cranes that, as long as the actors were filmed from the waist up, would make them seem to be floating about their spacecraft. Bacon would spend at least part of his time on a drifting, spinning bellyboard that would allow him to achieve the same effect but in a prone or supine position. Each time filming stopped to allow one or another piece of this equipment to be set up or repositioned, the costly, power-consuming refrigeration system would have to be briefly turned off. Each time the shot resumed, the air handlers and the dreaded misters would be turned back on.

With dozens of scenes in *Apollo 13* scripted for inside the frigid spacecraft, the cast and crew knew that their stay on Stage 34 would be as long as thirty days—or about twenty-seven days longer than the Apollo 13 astronauts were forced to endure such near-freezing conditions. With the far more temperate climate of southern California just outside the door, nobody associated with the filming pretended that their ordeal was anything like what the genuine astronauts suffered. Nobody, however, pretended they had ever experienced anything like it either.

"I can't wait to hear what people say when this movie comes out," said a bone-chilled Tom Hanks, leaning against the wall outside the stage and trying to warm up between takes. "You just know they're going to look at the condensation coming out of our mouths and say, 'I guess they found a big, walk-in refrigerator and had the astronauts and the director work in there for a few days. I mean, they wouldn't do something ridiculous like, oh, refrigerate a *whole* set.'"

11

The Men in Charge: Ron Howard and Gene Kranz

Ron Howard and Gene Kranz have more in common than either of them would once have thought. The Apollo 13 flight director and the *Apollo 13* film director came of age in different eras, worked in different fields, and learned different skills, but when it came to America's most dramatic lunar mission, their career arcs unexpectedly converged. The business of overseeing a flight to the moon may have more life-and-death implications than re-creating that flight on film, but in terms of the need to muster talent, coordinate resources, and bring an inexpressibly complex project to fruition, the two jobs are more similar than dissimilar. During the course of the *Apollo 13* project, Howard and Kranz sat down for individual interviews with me in which they discussed a wide range of topics, including their lives, their work, America's past and future in space, and what both of them learned from the Apollo 13 experience.

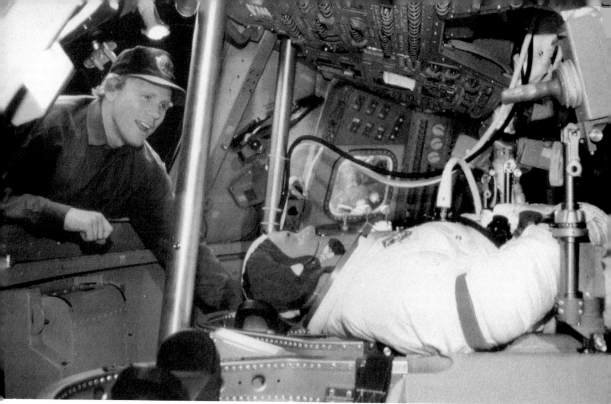
Ron Howard directing Tom Hanks in the simulated command module.

On the highest and lowest points in NASA's history:
Where were you at the moment of the Apollo 1 fire and the Apollo 11 lunar landing?

Howard: The fire was in January of 1967, so I was twelve when it happened, just going on thirteen. I was working on the *Andy Griffith Show* at the time, so it was tough for me to follow every space flight as it happened. Instead, I followed the whole program in a sort of broad, big-picture way. Traveling in space seemed to me like something the country *ought* to be doing, something it was *right* for us to be doing. When the Apollo 1 astronauts were killed, I don't remember doubting that we would continue doing it. Certainly, I was saddened—everybody was. But I don't remember thinking that it would call into question the whole idea of space travel.

Apollo 11 was a much clearer memory. I had been working on a movie for Disney and went over to the home of the director, a man named Vince McAveety. He was having a lunar-landing party like the one we have in *Apollo 13*. I remember being out back at his house sort of goofing around

Dave Scott with Ron Howard in Mission Control.

when somebody called out to us and said that it was about to happen—Neil Armstrong was about to walk on the moon. I ran inside and there was Walter Cronkite on TV, and suddenly there Armstrong was, too. I was incredibly proud. I couldn't believe we had done it and I couldn't believe the next step wouldn't be Mars.

As dramatic as both Apollo 1 and Apollo 11 were, the thing that really impressed me most was the first space walk [in 1964, by Ed White, one of the men killed in the fire]. I was stunned by that. I remember the articles in the *Weekly Reader* saying that we'd all be flying in our own spacecraft soon like in *The Jetsons*. Back then it seemed so possible. I was all set.

Kranz: As I recall, I found out about the Apollo 1 fire like anyone else. I wasn't scheduled to work the launch rehearsal that night, so I think I was just driving down the Gulf Freeway taking my wife out to dinner. We turned on the radio and we heard the astronauts had been killed. I don't even remember if I said anything or not; I just turned the car around, went straight home, and then came directly over to the control center to see what was happening.

For Apollo 11, I was working as flight director in the MOCR for much of the mission, including the landing. A lot of people remember the actual lunar touchdown as very smooth, but in fact, we had some pretty tense moments. Shortly before landing, we had a series of computer alarms known as 1201 and 1202 alarms. Essentially, these are the computer's way of telling the crew and the ground, 'Hey, I'm too busy to do everything you're telling me to do, so I'm going to take care of just the higher-priority items first.' Under these conditions, the computer's still running, but in a saturated state. We knew that if it went on that way for too long, it would just stop, which could have meant the end of our primary guidance for descent.

At the same time this was happening, the guidance officer recognized that

The splashdown scene being filmed.

we had a downrange trajectory error that was causing us to move toward what we called the toe of the footprint—the far forward end of the landing site. This would have put us directly in a boulder field. All we had was about a minute and a half of propellant left, and pretty soon that was down to sixty seconds and then forty-five seconds and then thirty seconds. It was pretty tense for a while, and then somebody came on the loop and said, 'Hey, it's just like a simulation.' After that, everybody just sort of relaxed, and Armstrong managed to set the LEM down fine.

On astronauts as American heroes:
When working with men who have traveled to the moon, do you ever find yourself stepping back and reflecting on the enormity of what these people have accomplished?

Howard: What I took away from my first meetings with Jim Lovell, Dave Scott, and the other Apollo astronauts I met was that while these guys are uniquely focused individuals, they're also very much regular guys. Certainly, they're extremely gifted. They are honestly the first people I've ever met who could wear me down in a meeting. They seem to have no fatigue level. They apply themselves intellectually like nobody I've ever met. But despite that, you also can't help but be pleasantly surprised that you're not dealing with supermen. What you are dealing with are qualified human beings who dedicated themselves to a goal—going to the moon—and then went out and figured out how to do it. You can almost take it the next step and say, "Gee, maybe I could have done that." Early on, I made the decision to try to capture that accessibility, that very normality of film—and I think we were able to.

Of course, having said all that, I have to admit that sometimes I've been in a meeting with Jim or Dave and I've pinched myself and said, "I'm talking to one of the remarkable people of the twentieth century." I think everyone associated with *Apollo 13* has enjoyed that experience at one point or another.

Kranz: Mostly, people who work in Mission Control respect astronauts as exceptional pilots. During an emergency like Apollo 13, you *count* on them to be. As a pilot myself, I know that one of your first jobs in any crisis is to protect your options—to preserve as many as you can while closing down others. If you can't achieve your initial goals, can you achieve lesser ones? Eventually, those goals may come down to mere survival, but even then, you don't let yourself doubt that you can accomplish them, because once you do, you lose the mental sharpness, the mental edge that's going to take a survival situation and bring it to a successful conclusion.

I think I drove the press nuts during Apollo 13 because of how completely I subscribed to that philosophy. There was never any question about my confidence in our hardware or our ability or the astronauts' ability to bring the spacecraft back to Earth. I remember one reporter asked if I thought we were going to be able to get the crew home and I snapped, "Look, it's not a question of *if* we're gonna get them home. It's a question of when we're gonna get them home and how much of the spacecraft we're gonna have left when we do." The reporter turned to the guy next to him and said, "Arrogant son of a bitch, isn't he?"

On running the show:
In an operation as complex as directing a movie or directing a space flight, how absolute is the authority of the person in charge?

Howard: A NASA flight director has the responsibility of keeping the entire mission objective in mind and knowing enough to ask when something is drifting off course. It's never a one-man band. He's working with world-class technicians and wants to draw from their experience to maximize the likelihood of achieving the central objective. In a sense, that's what a movie director does, too. Often, you don't have the answer in your hip pocket and you have to defer to the wisdom of one of the other people involved in the project. Thankfully, national objectives like the future of manned space flight don't rest on the decisions I make, but the process of making those decisions is still quite similar.

Of course, ultimately every director has to bear the final responsibility for what goes on in shooting a movie. In *Apollo 13,* this was especially true when it came to filming our weightlessness scenes. If I had really understood before going into it what was involved in shooting in the KC-135, I might have backed away from it. There were financial issues to consider; there were logistical issues, like how we were going to make the set fit inside the confines of the plane, to consider; there was the simple question of whether it really was possible to stage the scenes we wanted to stage in a zero-g environment to consider. At a certain point I just said if the actors are willing to give it a try, I'm willing to. If it works, it's unprecedented; if it doesn't, it doesn't. I certainly wasn't on an irrational mission, but I also knew that no matter how wonderful the special-effects wizards working on the movie were, there was no way simulated weightlessness would look as good as the real thing.

Kranz: During any mission, especially one like Apollo 13, one of the biggest jobs of the flight director is to ask the individual controllers questions and get things moving in the right direction. A lot of the discussions involve little more than, "Guidance, do you have a solution to our trajectory problems? . . . Okay, go down and talk to FIDO and work it out with him. Once you've figured out where it's going to fit in the flight plan, come back and talk to me. . . . EECOM, you've got a power solution? . . . Fine." There were so many piece parts that had to come together, there was no time to dwell on any one of them. The only thing I did dwell on was the use of time, because we knew we had to fit within certain windows. If you don't do something and make the maneuver at this time, you're going to be flying by the Earth and then you've lost the ball game.

During Apollo 13—and, for that matter, every flight—there were a lot of intense discussions like this between the flight director and the controllers. With flight-dynamics guys like Jerry Bostick or Phil Schaffer, the conversa-

The real-life Jim Lovell with Bill Paxton and Kevin Bacon on the recovery ship.

tions would get especially intense. Sometimes, in the evenings during the months between missions, we would all sit around a keg of beer in the King's Inn in Houston and talk about mission techniques. The FIDOs didn't expect us flight directors to understand everything they were talking about, and we didn't. The mathematical aspects, the Keplerian equations, the exquisite motions of the sun and moon and the Earth—flight directors couldn't care less about that. The Earth's down below us, that's where we come back to land; that's the sort of footing we started off with, and we left a lot of the other stuff to the people responsible for the trajectory design in the first place. You have to have this kind of faith in your controllers, otherwise you could never get any mission off the ground.

On Apollo 13 as both history and drama:
Do you think people have ever fully appreciated the magnitude of the crisis Apollo 13 faced?

Howard: When a director initially considers doing a movie like *Apollo 13*, the first thought is often, "Well, we might have to crank it up a bit. We'll *base* it on what really happened, but we'll Hollywoodize it." What really happened in Apollo 13, however, was so suspenseful and entertaining and fresh, it required no Hollywoodizing. As a storyteller, I found that what differentiated *Apollo 13* from a science fiction movie or a cop movie or most other movies was that if you were trying to determine which direction to take your plot, you didn't have to agonize very much; all you had to do was fall back on historical fact. What you see when you go back to the Apollo era are these comparatively primitive missions run by comparatively primitive computers that have been eclipsed by today's pocket calculators. It makes what they were trying to accomplish seem that much more ambitious and a crisis like Apollo 13 seem that much more dramatic. I didn't quite understand how touch and go the mission was until I started studying it. Once I did, I knew we had a terrific story on our hands.

Kranz: As a result of our training we were always conditioned to believe that there was some way out of any box that we had gotten ourselves into. After the explosion aboard Apollo 13, I remember going into the operations room with [Flight Director] Glynn Lunney and [Assistant NASA Administrator] Chris Kraft and the three of us coming to an almost intuitive conclusion that we had a problem of sufficient severity that our only option was to come home. We didn't know the extent of the damage to the service module, but we knew we could not trust it functionally to do its job.

One of the first things I had to do after that realization was to get the flight controllers on my team together and address that fact formally. I'm sort of a direct guy, so in a situation like this I would sit down with them and try to lay out what I really expected of them, what the time frame for resolution was, and get them basically thinking about the urgency of the problem. In a bind like this, the trick is to get everybody focusing totally on what the issue is as opposed to the consequences. If everybody worries, "Well, if this thing happens or this thing happens," you're not going to solve anything. Our job is to *make* things happen. It's a question of achieving the positive frame of mind that is necessary to work problems out in a time-critical, emergency environment.

The past as prologue:
What will be the enduring lesson of either the mission or the movie of Apollo 13?

Kranz: I suppose what we learned from Apollo 13 is that the training protocols we use in preparing for space flight are good ones. When a ground team is being assembled and trained, the simulation supervisors watch our process of preparation, poke holes in us as a team and, in general, determine if we have the ability to make crisp decisions and work together efficiently. By the time that process is finished, the team should have come together, established their strengths and weaknesses, and developed an attitude that's so positive that, given a few seconds, they can basically solve any problem thrown out to them. What you're essentially trying to achieve in these situations is the perfection of people relations, the perfection of technical relations, the perfection of preparedness and everything else. Those are the kinds of things you've got going for you in any crisis, and those are the kinds of things that allowed Apollo 13 to come home safely.

Howard: It might be grandiose to suggest that a movie, by itself, can have an impact on the future of manned space flight. What *is* possible, perhaps, is that one day some great space pioneer will remember seeing this film and perhaps remember having been affected by it. The more the story is told, I believe, the more it becomes a part of our culture and the more it helps preserve the sensibility that was behind the Apollo program. I don't doubt that making a movie about Apollo 13 was a lot more fun than flying it, but there was still a heavy responsibility associated with it. Months or years from now, none of us wanted to look in the mirror and say we didn't do this remarkable story justice.

AFTERWORD

O n July 21, 1994—twenty-five years and one day after the Apollo 11 lunar landing—I was walking through the lobby of the Ambassador Hotel in Los Angeles with Ron Howard and a production team from Imagine Films. There was a time when the Ambassador was the zenith of hotel luxury. The pile in the lobby carpets could fairly swallow you up; the fabrics in the ballroom drapes hung lush and heavy; the chandeliers throughout the place seemed able to light a city.

That time is now long gone. It was several years ago that the once-magnificent Ambassador welcomed its last guest and closed down its last room. There was talk that the old Ambassador would be refurbished and reopened as a newer, better Ambassador, that it would be converted into a condominium residence, that it would be razed to rubble to make room for some other business. Nobody, it seemed, was certain what the Ambassador's future would be and, for Hollywood filmmakers at least, that wasn't such a bad thing. For some time now, directors and location scouts in search of a good spot to shoot a bedroom, drawing room, or conference room scene had found that the faded landmark offered just the thing. Splash a little fresh paint on the walls, cart some new furniture in, and the cameras couldn't ask for a friendlier place.

On that summer day in 1994, Howard and his team were hunting for a room in which to film the opening scene of the soon-to-be-shot *Apollo 13,* the scene in which five bleary, unshaven astronauts gather in a Georgetown hotel suite to discuss the deaths of three of their friends in the Apollo 1 fire the night before. The Ambassador today was an eerie place to be—its rooms lit mostly by shafts of raw sunlight, its floors and walls emitting the occasional creaks of an old ocean liner at anchor. Nobody in the Imagine crew, however, seemed to be paying much attention to the surroundings. What they were thinking and talking about were the people involved in the real-life Apollo 13 mission. And the person they were talking about the most was Gene Kranz.

The night before, on the quarter-century anniversary of Apollo 11's triumphant lunar landing, public television and WGBH TV in Boston had broadcast a documentary not about that monumentally successful mission, but about the near-disastrous one that followed two flights later. Jim Lovell, the commander of Apollo 13, had been interviewed extensively; so had Fred Haise, his surviving crewmate; and so had many of the men who labored so valiantly in Mission Control during that week in April 1970.

At least a hundred controllers in rotating shifts had manned the two dozen consoles in the giant auditorium over the 141-hour mission, surrendering their stations when their eight-hour stints were up, but rarely moving more than a few feet away lest the man they had yielded to needed a key bit of data that would help out in a crucial moment. Of all of the controllers who had worked so hard in the Houston complex, there was none who had worked harder or on whom more responsibility rested than lead flight director Gene Kranz.

With his Air Force look and his Air Force mien, Kranz, an ex–Korean War aviator, had come to NASA more than a decade earlier, and he quickly learned to run the Mission Control auditorium with the crispness and confidence with which he would have run a platoon. There were three other flight directors who worked the Apollo 13 mission—Gerry Griffin, Glynn Lunney, and Milt Windler—as well as additional ones who were assigned to other flights, and while nobody questioned the skills of any of them, nobody pretended that the fiercely focused Gene Kranz was not the greatest of all of these gifted equals.

Kranz had been among the mission controllers appearing on the PBS program, and if the years had been both kind and unkind to most of the men on the screen, they seemed to have left Kranz alone. The set of the 60-plus-year-old jaw seemed unchanged; the staccato speech rhythms seemed unsmoothed; the military buzz cut, chosen more than a generation and a half ago, appeared not to have grown by more than a centimeter.

But if the external Kranz seemed impervious to the march of time, the internal Kranz seemed a bit less so. Near the end of the documentary, the former flight director, who had provided much of the technical commentary throughout the two-hour program, was asked just what feelings he took away with him from the Apollo 13 mission. Kranz, not given to this kind of gratuitous reflection, at first looked uncomfortable with the question. What did he take away with him? What *should* he take away with him? The men made it home, didn't they? Slowly, however, he began to reflect, and then to soften. He spoke of the atmosphere in Mission Control the moment the Apollo 13 spacecraft splashed down—how cigars were lit, hands were shaken, tiny American flags were broken out and waved by the jubilant men at their consoles.

All at once, utterly unexpectedly, Kranz, the unflappable Kranz, began to well up. Struggling mightily—*militarily*—to maintain his composure, he managed to summarize with brilliant understatement how he felt about what all of them had accomplished that week.

"It was . . ." he said haltingly, ". . . it was . . . neat."

It was that moment—those tears—that had most stayed with the people who had watched the program the night before. And in the gloaming of the Ambassador Hotel the next afternoon, it was those tears that Ron Howard and his Imagine crew were discussing.

"If we've got a story that can make Gene Kranz cry," somebody said, "we've got a story."

Howard smiled. He already knew he had a story. Now he had to set about telling it.

APPENDIX
The Apollo Missions

APOLLO 1

Crew: Gus Grissom, commander
Ed White, command module pilot
Roger Chaffee, lunar module pilot
Launched: Was not launched. The astronauts perished in a launch pad fire during a countdown dress rehearsal on January 27, 1967, just weeks before their scheduled launch.

APOLLO 2

Crew: None
Launched: July 5, 1967
Mission: A 224-foot tall, unmanned Saturn 1-B booster was launched to test the performance of its engines, the separation of its stages, and the ability of the cryogenic tanks to store supercold liquids in zero-g.

APOLLO 3

Crew: None
Launched: August 26, 1967
Mission: An unmanned Saturn 1-B was launched on a suborbital flight to test subsystems in the command and service modules, overall structural integrity of the vehicle, and the performance of the spacecraft's heat shield.

APOLLO 4

Crew: None
Launched: November 9, 1967
Mission: The first launch of the 363-foot Saturn 5 booster. The mission lasted eight and a half hours and included two orbits by an unmanned command-service module in order to test reentry techniques, heat shield performance, and numerous spacecraft systems.

APOLLO 5

Crew: None
Launched: January 22, 1968
Mission: A Saturn 1-B booster was launched in order to conduct the first flight tests of an unmanned lunar module.

APOLLO 6

Crew: None
Launched: April 4, 1968
Mission: Further testing of both the Saturn 5 booster and the Apollo command-service modules. While the spacecraft modules themselves performed well, the rocket as a whole did not, with two second-stage engines and the sole third-stage engine either failing to ignite or shutting down early. In addition, the rocket as a whole displayed a disturbing tendency to "pogo," oscillating back and forth as it climbed, with a repetitive motion reminiscent of a pogo stick.

APOLLO 7

Crew: Wally Schirra, commander
Donn Eisele, command module pilot
Walt Cunningham, lunar module pilot
Launched: October 11, 1968
Splashdown: October 21, 1968
Mission: First Earth-orbit test of the Apollo command-service module. No lunar module.

APOLLO 8

Crew: Frank Borman, commander
Jim Lovell, command module pilot
Bill Anders, lunar module pilot
Launched: December 21, 1968
Splashdown: December 27, 1968
Mission: First manned orbit of the moon. Command-service module only.

APOLLO 9

Crew: James A. McDivitt, commander
Dave Scott, command module pilot
Rusty Schweickart, lunar module pilot
Launched: March 3, 1969
Splashdown: March 13, 1969
Mission: First Earth-orbit test of both command-service module and lunar module.

APOLLO 10

Crew: Tom Stafford, commander
John Young, command module pilot
Gene Cernan, lunar module pilot
Launched: May 18, 1969
Splashdown: May 26, 1969
Mission: First test of both command-service module and lunar module in orbit around the moon. Stafford and Cernan pilot LEM to within 50,000 feet of the lunar surface.

APOLLO 11

Crew: Neil Armstrong, commander
Michael Collins, command module pilot
Buzz Aldrin, lunar module pilot
Launched: July 16, 1969
Splashdown: July 24, 1969
Mission: First lunar landing. Armstrong and Aldrin land in Sea of Tranquillity and spend 2 hours and 31 minutes walking on the moon. Collins orbits overhead in the command module.

APOLLO 12

Crew: Pete Conrad, commander
Dick Gordon, command module pilot
Alan Bean, lunar module pilot
Launched: November 14, 1969
Splashdown: November 24, 1969
Mission: Second lunar landing. Conrad and Bean land in Ocean of Storms, collect rocks and retrieve parts from unmanned Surveyor spacecraft, which landed nearby in April 1967.

APOLLO 13

Crew: Jim Lovell, commander
Jack Swigert, command module pilot
Fred Haise, lunar module pilot
Launched: April 11, 1970
Splashdown: April 17, 1970
Mission: Third attempted lunar landing. At 55 hours, 54 minutes, and 53 seconds into the mission, a cryogenic tank explodes, causing a loss of breathable oxygen and power in the command-service module. Crew abandons ship and survive in the LEM until just a few hours before splashdown, when they return to the command module, jettison the LEM, and re-enter the atmosphere.

APOLLO 14

Crew: Alan Shepard, commander
Stuart Roosa, command module pilot
Ed Mitchell, lunar module pilot
Launched: January 31, 1971
Splashdown: February 9, 1971
Mission: Third lunar landing. Shepard and

Mitchell touch down in the Fra Mauro highlands, the intended destination of Apollo 13.

APOLLO 15

Crew: David Scott, commander
Al Worden, command module pilot
Jim Irwin, lunar module pilot
Launched: July 26, 1971
Splashdown: August 7, 1971
Mission: Fourth lunar landing. Scott and Irwin touch down at Hadley Rille in the Apennine Mountains. First test of the four-wheel-drive lunar roving vehicle.

APOLLO 16

Crew: John Young, commander
Ken Mattingly, command module pilot
Charlie Duke, lunar module pilot
Launched: April 16, 1972
Splashdown: April 27, 1972
Mission: Fifth lunar landing. Young and Duke land in the Cayley-Descartes highlands, drive lunar roving vehicle 16.8 miles, and collect 213 pounds of lunar samples.

APOLLO 17

Crew: Gene Cernan, commander
Ron Evans, command module pilot
Harrison Schmitt, lunar module pilot
Launched: December 7, 1972
Splashdown: December 19, 1972
Mission: Sixth and last moon landing. Cernan and Schmitt touch down in the Taurus Mountains near the Littrow crater, collect 243 pounds of samples, and lift off from the lunar surface after seventy-five hours and three moonwalks.

GLOSSARY

Apollo spacecraft: When singular, generally refers to the command and service modules that the astronauts used to orbit Earth and the moon. When plural, refers to both the command-service modules and the lunar module.

Atlas booster: The 82-foot tall rocket used for Mercury missions in Earth orbit.

capcom: Controller who conducted all *air-to-ground* conversations with the spacecraft.

command module (CM): The conical cockpit in which the Apollo astronauts lived; the only part of the spacecraft to make it back to Earth.

CONTROL: Control officer; the mission controller who oversaw the trajectory of the lunar module.

EECOM: Environmental and electrical command officer; the mission controller who oversaw the spacecraft's power and life support systems.

FIDO: Flight dynamics officer; one of the mission controllers who oversaw spacecraft trajectory.

flight director: The overall boss of Mission Control.

Gemini spacecraft: The two-man vehicle that NASA used for its seventh through sixteenth manned missions, all in Earth orbit.

GNC: Guidance, navigation, and control officer; the mission controller who oversaw the hardware that controlled spacecraft trajectory.

GUIDO: Guidance officer; another mission controller who oversaw spacecraft trajectory.

INCO: Instrumentation and communications officer; the mission controller who oversaw spacecraft communications.

KC-135: A modified Boeing 707 used to simulate weightlessness.

LLTV: Lunar landing training vehicle; a four-legged hovercraft designed to help train astronauts to land their lunar module on the surface of the moon.

lunar excursion module (LEM): The four-legged lander in which two of the three Apollo astronauts descended to the surface of the moon.

Mercury spacecraft: The one-man vehicle that NASA used for its first six manned spaced missions.

Mission Control: The auditorium at the Manned Spacecraft Center in Houston where space flights were run.

MOCR: Mission Operations Control Room; another name for Mission Control.

Redstone booster: The 82-foot rocket used for Mercury suborbital missions.

RETRO: Retrofire officer; the mission controller who oversaw return to Earth and reentry.

S-1C: The first stage of the Saturn 5 rocket.

S-II: The second stage of the Saturn 5 rocket.

S-IVB: The third stage of the Saturn 5 rocket.

Saturn 1-B: The 224-foot two-stage booster used for most Apollo Earth orbit missions.

Saturn 5: The 363-foot three-stage booster used principally for Apollo lunar missions.

service module (SM): The cylindrical structure attached to the rear of the Apollo command module; the service module housed the spacecraft's engine and environmental systems and power-generating hardware.

Titan booster: The 108-foot rocket used for Gemini missions.

TELMU: Telemetry, electrical, EVA mobility unit officer; the mission controller responsible for the environmental and power systems in the lunar module.

Vomit Comet: A more colloquial—and certainly more accurate—name for the KC-135.

AUTHOR'S NOTES

On Christmas Eve nearly twenty-seven years ago, I, like tens of millions of other people, sat transfixed as the crew of Apollo 8 orbited the moon, beamed their tantalizingly grainy pictures of the surface of the distant world back to Earth, and read aloud—poignantly, poetically—from the book of Genesis. Sixteen months later, I returned to my television set, along with an even larger global audience, as Apollo 13, the third planned mission to the surface of the moon, suffered an explosion in its service module, imperiling the lives of its three-man crew, and setting into motion the most compelling drama in the history of manned space travel. In late 1991, I was privileged to make the acquaintance of Jim Lovell, the one man who flew aboard both of those ships, as we set about the job of writing the account of that second, harrowing mission: *Lost Moon: The Perilous Voyage of Apollo 13* (later retitled simply *Apollo 13*.)

The two years spent on the *Lost Moon* project, followed by an additional year of work on the *Apollo 13* movie based on the book, were unparalleled ones. Much of what I learned in that time—about the business of flying into space, the business of making movies, and the remarkable people who have dedicated their lives to doing both—is included in *The Apollo Adventure*.

The chapters devoted to the history of the lunar program were the most labor-intensive in the book, involving interviews with astronauts and flight controllers, visits to various NASA facilities around the country, and un-counted days spent with the documents, tapes, transcripts, and technical manuals stored in the NASA History Office in Washington, D.C. As in the *Apollo 13* book, the air-to-ground and cockpit conversations in *this* book were taken directly from official space agency transcripts, though in some cases those exchanges have been edited or paraphrased in the interests of both comprehensibility and readability. In no cases, however, has the substance or science of the dialogue been changed. Conversations that were not preserved on tape were reconstructed through interviews with at least one of the principals involved.

The *Apollo 13* movie chapters were a bit easier to compile, since most of the information came from the four extraordinary months I spent on the set of the movie while principal photography was under way. During post-produc-tion, a number of key people involved in the film—especially Ron Howard and Michael Bostick, of Imagine Films; Todd Hallowell, Executive Producer of *Apollo 13;* Rob Legato of Digital Domain; production designer Michael Corenblith; and Max Ary, of the Kansas Cosmosphere and Space Center—gave generously of their time so that lingering questions I had could be answered and additional information, not available through mere observation, could be included in the manuscript.

A book like *The Apollo Adventure* falls into the category of what the talented Tom Miller of Pocket Books taught me to call a crash book—one put together on an extraordinarily tight schedule in order to meet an extraordinarily tight deadline. Such a project would have been impossible without the aid of a number of people, including, of course, Tom himself. Among the others whose assistance was indispensable were numerous members of the NASA family, past and present, including Dave Scott, Gene Cernan, Jerry Bostick, Gerry Griffin, Chris Kraft, Sy Liebergot, and, as always, the extraordinarily helpful Lee Saegesser of the NASA History Office.

Also lending their help were the folks at MCA/Universal Studios in Los Angeles, especially Nancy Cushing-Jones, Liz Gengl, and Bette Einbinder.

The Apollo Adventure could never have been written, of course—and, indeed, the *Apollo 13* movie would never have been made—if not for the family of gifted men and women associated with Imagine Films and with the *Apollo 13* production itself. I've long since stopped counting the people I consider myself fortunate to have worked with in the past year, but the ones to whom I owe the greatest debt of gratitude are Ron Howard, whose graceful foreword to this book only begins to capture the sense of wonder and imagination he brought to the Apollo 13 story; and Brian Grazer, who recognized that that story needed to be told and committed the resources of Imagine Films to telling it. Thanks also go to Michael Bostick, Louisa Velis, Todd Hallowell, Karen Kehela, Julie Donatt, Erin McKeever Gaghan, Al Reinert, and Bill Broyles; as well as to Tom Hanks, for bringing such inspiration to the role of Jim Lovell; and to Eddee Kolos, for explaining to me—patiently—how a movie set works.

Finally, more appreciation than I can express goes to Jim Lovell, for his friendship and guidance, and for teaching me that the collaborative whole is greater than the sum of its parts. Equal thanks go to everyone at the Lantz-Harris Literary Agency, especially Leslie Daniels and Paul Chung, and most especially Joy Harris; if there is a better writer's advocate in all of the publishing world, there have yet to be any confirmed sightings.